THE DON'T SWEAT GUIDE
TO TRAVEL

Other books by the editors of Don't Sweat Press

The Don't Sweat Affirmations
The Don't Sweat Guide for Couples
The Don't Sweat Guide for Graduates
The Don't Sweat Guide for Grandparents
The Don't Sweat Guide for Parents
The Don't Sweat Guide for Moms
The Don't Sweat Guide for Weddings
The Don't Sweat Guide to Golf
The Don't Sweat Stories
The Don't Sweat Guide to Taxes
The Don't Sweat Guide to Weight Loss

THE DON'T SWEAT GUIDE TO TRAVEL

Hitting the Road Without Excess Worry

By the Editors of Don't Sweat Press
Foreword by Richard Carlson, Ph.D.,
author of the bestselling *Don't Sweat the Small Stuff*

HYPERION

New York

ISBN: 0-7868-8811-3

FIRST EDITION

10 9 8 7 6 5 4 3 2 1

Contents

Foreword   11

1. Getting Away from It All   15

2. Where in the World?   17

3. Just Around the Corner   19

4. Agents' Secrets   21

5. Web Travel   23

6. Rock-Bottom Deals to Top Travel Destinations   26

7. The Train or the Plane?   29

8. To "E" or Not to "E"?   31

9. Top Five Vacation Ideas for Singles   33

10. Top Five Vacation Ideas for Couples   35

11. Top Five Vacation Ideas for Families   37

12. Top Five Vacation Ideas for Seniors   40

13. Big Plans, Little Cash   43

14. Not-So-Frequent Fliers   46

15. Arriving Stress-Free   48

16. Airplane Kiddie Bag   51

17. Travel Safety   53

18. What to Pack?   56

19. Choosing the Perfect Paperback   58

20. Ten Things to Pack for Stress-Free Travel   60

21. Don't Pack the Whole Medicine Cabinet   62

22. How to Leave Your House   64

23. Did I Leave the Oven On?   66

24. Leaving the Kids Behind   68

25. Party of Twenty-Seven   70

26. No Children Allowed   72

27. Airports 101   74

28. Car Rental Reality   77

29. Surviving the Family Road Trip   79

30. When Nature Calls   81

31. The Perfect Family Vacation   83

32. Traveling Alone   85

33. The Importance of Being Prepared   87

34. Traveling on the Fly   89

35. All-Inclusive, or All-Intrusive?   90

36. Cruise Control   92

37. Unconventional Vacations   93

38. Surviving Theme Parks   95

39. Map Savvy   97

40. Day Trippers   98

41. Organize Your Day Bag   100

42. Getting What You Paid For   102

43. Holiday Travel Without the Horror   105

44. Combating Jet Lag   107

45. How to Do…Nothing!   109

46. There's No Business Like a Business Trip!   111

47. More Unconventional Vacations   113

48. First Class Act   115

49. Taking Kitty Along   117

50. Are Traveler's Checks a Thing of the Past?   120

51. Memorizing the Exchange Rate 122

52. Are You Euro-Ready? 124

53. Où Est la Restroom? 126

54. Off the Beaten Path 128

55. Don't Stress over a Change of Plans 130

56. Your Extended Stay 132

57. "Are We There Yet?" 134

58. The Perfect Unpacking 136

59. Lost Luggage Anxiety 138

60. The Sightseeing Checklist 141

61. "The Louvre, Again?" 143

62. Dining Out with Kids 145

63. Bed, Breakfast, and Bliss 148

64. What Is Montezuma's Revenge? 150

65. A Table for Four 152

66. Self-Timers Are a Must! 154

67. Together 24/7 157

68. Just the Two of Us 159

69. How to Screen the Hotel Baby-Sitter   161

70. Festival Occasions   163

71. Time-Sharing   165

72. It's All Relative   167

73. Functioning Without the Minivan   169

74. Driving in a Foreign Country   171

75. Away from Homeland Security   173

76. First-Aid on the Go   175

77. Are You Prepared for an Emergency?   177

78. Indulge in Room Service   180

79. Here's a Tip…   182

80. Understanding the Locals   184

81. Have Fun!   186

82. The Art of Shopping on Vacation   188

83. Take a Vacation from Your Vacation   190

84. Rules for Parents   192

85. Writing It All Down   194

86. Put Down the Video Camera   196

87. Unconventional Souvenirs 197

88. Lugging Luggage That You Like 199

89. To Go or Not to Go? 201

90. Stress in the Sky 203

91. The Vacation Five 205

92. Surfside Safety 207

93. Travel Fraud 209

94. The Hotel Stairmaster 211

95. Winding Down 213

96. The Night-Before Checklist 215

97. Don't Carry It…Ship It 218

98. Hello, Airport Gift Shop! 220

99. Your Vacation Scrapbook 221

100. Home at Last…I Could Use a Vacation! 223

Foreword

What a perfect time to read this book! Travel certainly isn't what it used to be. With increased security at airports, more crowded freeways, and busy, hurried travelers everywhere we look, we all need a way to keep our perspective and build a reservoir of patience.

Travel is one of those aspects of life that can be, and often is, inherently stressful. Whether it's a busy airport bustling with impatient travelers, or a crowded airplane, air travel can be difficult and frustrating. There are often mechanical or weather-related delays as well.

Traffic jams, accidents, and angry drivers make driving a nail-biting experience. Trains, buses, and ferries are subject to delays and other problems. Restaurants and hotel lobbies can be crowded and loud. All over the world, there are pushy, sometimes obnoxious people, some of them driving taxicabs! What's a person to do?

The editors of Don't Sweat Press offer us a great partial solution. This book is filled with powerful ideas designed to ease the stress of travel. While no one can take away all the hassles inherent in travel—packing, planning, spending money, being in crowds, getting lost, experiencing bad weather, being delayed or stranded, getting sick, and so many other things—we can learn healthier ways in which to view such problems.

This book offers some sound advice on taking it more in stride. It helps us learn to minimize the hassles we face, while at the same time accepting those that are inevitable. In this way, we can focus less on the inconvenience of travel, and remember instead the joys and benefits.

I was standing in a long ticket line at the airport. It appeared unlikely that anyone in my section of the line was going to make his or her flight. The entire scene was very chaotic, and many people were getting increasingly impatient. An older man in front me started to laugh. Someone else in the line asked him, "What's so funny, sir?" His reply made me think he had read this book. He said with a smile on his face, "When you step back from it, you have to admit it's a little bit funny. All these people taking it Oh so seriously. A few hours from now, we will all be where we need to be."

Being a seasoned traveler myself, I can appreciate the wisdom you're about to read. This book has given me new ammunition in my fight against irritation and impatience! I hope the next time you travel, whether for business or pleasure, the words in this book provide much needed comfort. Have a great trip!

Richard Carlson
Benicia, California
March 2002

THE DON'T SWEAT GUIDE TO TRAVEL

1.

Getting Away
from It All

Remember when getting away from it all amounted to a quick retreat to the shore or a weekend away in the mountains? Escaping to places like the Caribbean or even Europe seemed impossible due to expense, distance, limited air travel—and the popular notion that overseas vacations were something saved for special occasions.

But sometime during the 1980s, "getting away from it all" travel by Americans jumped nearly 70 percent, and more recently, pre-September 11, 2001, quick trips abroad accounted for more than half of all U.S. travel.

It isn't hard to see why. Heavy work schedules for both partners in a relationship or family have made it harder to plan long vacations. But it's those same heavy work schedules, in addition to more family responsibilities than ever before, that give us more just cause for vacations in the first place!

Thankfully, with travel deals abounding, the dream of relaxation and rejuvenation abroad is being realized by more and more Americans—even for the short duration of a weekend. In fact, what's become more common these days, in light of a new era in travel, is forgoing the standard weeklong vacation and replacing it with multiple, extended weekend vacations. Exotic vacations have become more financially and logistically accessible.

The airline and travel industry have adapted to accommodate the public. Deregulation, frequent flier miles, time-sharing packages, "open skies" agreements allowing more flights between countries, the introduction of lower-cost air carriers, and a greater number of direct flights, have made it all less of a burden for Americans to spend their precious vacation time—short- or long-term—almost anywhere. It makes more and more sense these days to get away from it all—and take advantage of what the rest of the world has to offer.

2.

Where in the World?

Deciding just where to go may be the hardest aspect of planning a vacation nowadays. With literally thousands of fabulous destinations to choose from, how do you go about narrowing it down?

Naturally, everything depends on what it is you're looking for in a vacation: a warm or cool climate, a trek through ancient ruins, or a steady stream of museum visits. Perhaps you're after a vacation that encompasses it all.

Your best plan of action is to think carefully about your needs and wishes, make your decision, and run with it! The earlier you plan, the more opportunities will be available to you. Start researching your options the moment you get that vacation urge: Go online, visit your local library and bookstore, call the state or national tourist office of your destination, and collect any and all information about where you want to go.

It's fine to "fly by the seat of your pants" and remain flexible while on vacation, but preparing an itinerary before you leave can be helpful in preventing many vacation disasters—whether you're planning on a weeklong cruise to the Caribbean or just headed down to Miami to visit relatives. With an itinerary, you'll be sure to include ample time (and money) for yourself while weeding out the activities in which you have no interest. Best of all, by presenting any relatives with your travel plans beforehand, *they'll* be able to prepare for your visit as well, and the conflicts of interest and scheduling faux pas will be minimal.

Base your itinerary on your own interests and the interests of your traveling companions. If you and your spouse are turned off by crowds, take into consideration the season that you'll be visiting your destination as well.

Make sure the places that you want to visit will be open when you get there, and find out what the weather will be like. Pick a place where everyone in your group will have fun, especially if you're traveling with kids. That may mean adjusting your itinerary to include visiting child-friendly places each day. There's nothing worse than traveling with bored children. Though you and your spouse might find it fascinating to visit every art museum in Paris, your kids probably won't share your interest.

If you are still undecided and having trouble pleasing everyone, hit the newsstand and let the popular, tried-and-true vote decide your next vacation for you. Many top travel magazines poll the vacationing public and publish the results for the world's top picks for getaway destinations!

3.

Just Around
the Corner

Believe it or not, sometimes the best vacations are those spent within a few miles of home. It may be hard to think of planning a whole day around visiting the attractions that you pass daily on your way to work, or while dropping your kids off at school, but think about it: Aren't those the same places that millions of tourists flock to see each year? Many of us have even chosen our homes because of their close proximity to these popular attractions or historical landmarks—yet we never find the time to pay them a visit. Many of us live in or near great cities and within driving distance of national parks, popular amusement areas, or towns famous for local attractions.

It's important that you take a closer look at the places of interest in your own backyard the next time you plan a vacation. These are the places that you couldn't wait to visit when you first moved in. The quaint, old-fashioned ice cream factory, the birthplace of a former president—or any of the spectacular museums, beaches, lakes, spas, restaurants, or historical landmarks that are right around the corner! With a little effortless planning (a few local phone calls), you can find the best times to go, and perhaps you'll learn of some inexpensive hotels or inns in the area. The act of packing and staying at a hotel embodies so much of what we call "the spirit of vacation"—why not add to the fun by staying at a local hotel? You'll save on airfare, put very little mileage on your car, and still feel as though you "got away"!

4.

Agents' Secrets

With the World Wide Web right at your fingertips, you may wonder why hiring a travel agent to plan your next vacation makes sense. After all, you can certainly visit the popular travel sites on your own, and with a credit card and a calendar handy, book the entire thing yourself. The benefit? Saving money. The downside? What you save in money will cost you in terms of time and stress. It comes down to this: Which do you have more of, money or time?

There are a few things that you should know before you click yourself and your family away for the week. These secrets for navigating through all of the junk found on the Web are the expertise of experienced travel agents. Phony sites, fraudulent agencies, and good old-fashioned technical difficulties can frustrate the do-it-yourself vacation process to no end.

Does it make more sense to just call an agency and let the agent handle the entire thing? In some cases, yes. Professionals can be a valuable resource, sharing experiences and expertise. In addition, they are aware of the constantly changing discounts, promotions, and special deals. A good travel agent will have all of the latest information on new resorts and airlines. A *great* travel agent will also have a keen knowledge of local airports—rules and regulations that could have the less-knowledgeable running around in circles at the baggage claim for hours, and ruining a trip before it's even begun.

Travel agents rely on a commission from the airlines, hotels, cruise lines, and vacation resorts that they promote and sell—that's how they make their money. Sometimes, they charge the consumer directly for special situations, like arranging a complicated itinerary or handling large groups.

With this knowledge, you can make an educated choice as to which is ultimately more important to you when planning your next vacation. Just remember this: Whether you use a travel agent or choose to book your trip on your own, one thing is definite. If you don't ask for the best deal, the lowest price, the upgrade, the extended stay, or the complimentary breakfast, you won't get it!

5.

Web Travel

Although using the Internet to book a vacation is time-consuming, it is nonetheless a truly great resource for vacation planning. If you know what to look for when vacation shopping on the Internet, the experience can be rewarding.

The Internet has many travel web sites offering travel-related services, but they change or disappear quite frequently. It's estimated that there are over 10,000 travel sites currently out there! To know which ones are trustworthy, utilize the most popular travel sites when planning your vacation, and never give your credit card number to a web site that you haven't thoroughly investigated.

The Web has become a sophisticated research tool that can point out remote and exotic spots that you never knew existed. It's important, however, to prepare yourself before you log on, and remember that a visit to the 'Net doesn't always guarantee the best price for anything. The time you put into research is what *will* guarantee the best price.

Begin by creating columns on a sheet of paper or in a computer file where you can record all of the information for each airline or hotel. Then visit airline and hotel web sites and check the going rates for the dates that you plan to travel. You can find any number of these dot-coms by using a search engine to locate "travel" sites. You'll have a better idea of average prices when you begin to negotiate — or in the case of some sites, name your own price for travel.

Be wary of the rules and regulations for the travel site that you choose. For instance, naming your own airfare or hotel rate sounds great if the site accepts your crazy lowball offer, but you may have to take connecting flights. Usually, the more connections to which you agree, the lower the airfare.

Before making any reservations through the Internet, check the site that you are using with the Better Business Bureau. Visit the BBB site before providing any credit card information online and check the company's status and profile. You'll be able to learn if the site you're shopping on has any consumer complaints against it.

Though you should definitely proceed with caution, booking a vacation on the Internet can be a fun, rewarding, and informative experience. Often, travel services and online magazines can provide you with a wealth of information about your preferred destination and offer great suggestions toward making the most of your time there. You can also find links to other areas of interest related to your vacation, like a general public ratings system for certain tours or restaurants. In some cases, you can even arrange restaurant reservations, theater tickets, and tours through the same web site that you're booking your trip through.

Once you've confirmed your travel plans online, always save and print your receipt. This will be the only official paperwork and record of your itinerary that you have should something go wrong. But for the most part, travel purchased through the Internet runs smoothly. If it didn't, we wouldn't see Americans spending *billions* of dollars on Internet travel purchases each year!

6.

Rock-Bottom Deals
to Top Travel Destinations

There's nothing more stressful than sitting next to somebody on an airplane and learning that that person paid a lot less for his or her airline ticket than you paid for yours. Unfortunately, the average traveler isn't aware of the vast array of options when purchasing an airline or cruise ticket, or booking a hotel room. The fares and rates change frequently, and all vendors would prefer to sell you their tickets and rooms at their higher rates!

There is hope, however. You can educate yourself. There may be different fares for the exact same airplane seats in coach class. Here's why: Each fare is identified by a code letter, and each letter has a different rule. One fare may require a thirty-day advance purchase, a Saturday night stay-over, and a fifty percent penalty if the trip is cancelled. A higher fare for the same seat may be part of a deal that is purchased two days in advance but is also nonrefundable. It also matters which days of the week you choose to fly—Tuesday and Wednesday are usually the cheapest days to travel, Friday and Sunday the most expensive.

So how do you go about getting the rock-bottom fare? Always ask for the cheapest rates. That information is unlikely to be offered otherwise. Ask if traveling on a certain day is cheaper, or if there is another date for travel that would bring the fare down. When booking a cruise, ask about discounts for booking early, or promotions that include free airfare when booking; or choose a less expensive cabin—you'll still get the same great cruise service as the people who pay top-dollar.

Some hotels will eat up most of your total travel budget. A good piece of advice is to book a room for your first night of stay. Then once you're there, you can check out the smaller, neighborhood hotels for much better rates.

If you're looking for low, low travel rates, however, the important thing is to be flexible. For the best hotel rates, don't dial the hotel chain's 800 number, but call the hotel itself and negotiate your own rate. Remember that an unsold hotel room represents lost revenue for the hotel.

Can you travel with just one carry-on piece of luggage? Then a courier flight might be the way to go. Courier flights—though they have certain drawbacks—can cut your flying costs considerably. You're usually at the mercy of the courier company as to the dates of travel and length of stay, but reputable courier services offer flights to faraway destinations for a fraction of the fare. If you're *really* flexible, you may want to consider a charter flight. Charter flights are cheaper than regularly scheduled flights because you're becoming part of a group of seats on a flight rather than just purchasing one or two tickets.

Other great deals can be found through consolidators—or airline ticket brokers—who buy blocks of tickets to sell at a discount to individual travelers. You can save fifty percent on these seats that would otherwise remain unsold, but to find them, you'll need to do a bit of research through your newspaper's classified section.

Standby fares, travel clubs, smaller airlines, and even secondary airports are all ways to cut airfare costs, but keep in mind that these deals work best for solo travelers. A better bet for a vacationing family would be to find travel bargains through the Internet. Wherever you go for reservations, ask that all the possibilities be investigated before committing to a flight.

7.

The Train
or the Plane?

For those who are squeamish about flying, there is an alternative: rail travel. If time is on your side and you can afford to arrive at your destination a day or two later, railroad travel can introduce you to a new and relaxing way to go! In Europe, in fact, many prefer to travel by train than by plane.

Traveling by rail is a comfortable, scenic experience. In the United States, Amtrak offers luxury trains with sleeper cars on routes along some of the most breathtaking vistas in the country. Rail companies offer attractive family packages, reasonable rates, and the ability to take your car along.

For travel throughout Europe, the Eurail pass has always been an excellent deal. Favored for years by students traveling abroad, the Eurail pass is also a terrific way vacationers can visit many countries and cover a wider span of territory with just one ticket—plus you don't need a reservation to travel. You can wake up in Greece and decide you'd like to have dinner that night in Italy. With a Eurail pass, you can just head to the train station, find an unreserved seat, and show the conductor your pass. (If you want a reserved seat or a sleeper car, you need to secure a reservation in advance.) These passes also include travel by boat and ferry between certain countries. Eurail pass holders also enjoy great discounts on car rentals in some countries. The only thing you'll need to do is to purchase your Eurail pass in the United States—it costs a lot more once you're abroad.

If you're anxious over your next vacation because of flying, consider "railing" instead. It takes longer, but when you factor in your arrival in a calm, collected, and refreshed state, it stands to reason that your vacation will get off to a great start!

8.
To "E" or
Not to "E"?

Back in the 1990s when e-tickets were first introduced, consumers thought that they were getting something truly convenient and wonderful. How great it sounded in theory: Make a reservation and then just show up at the airport gate, show photo ID, and board the flight. No paper ticket to bother with, no fear of losing the ticket…no hassles at all!

In truth, the introduction of the e-ticket was primarily to reduce distribution costs for the airline. And though it *does* cut some time off an airport line, many travelers have found over the years that the e-ticket is not as wonderful as the airlines would have you believe.

For example, if a flight is delayed or cancelled, an e-ticket passenger will need to wait on a long line of unhappy travelers looking to rebook their flights, only to receive the basic paper ticket he or she had earlier avoided. A passenger needs the actual paper ticket to rebook on another airline—or even to get another flight on the same airline.

If you possess a paper ticket to begin with, you can just head over to the nearest ticket counter to rebook your flight on another airline. E-ticket holders run the risk of losing a seat on a new flight because of having to wait on the line that issues paper tickets.

Airline ticket computers have been programmed to automatically issue e-tickets, so you'll have to make a special request for a paper ticket from the airline or travel agent the next time that you fly. Be sure to pay for your ticket with a credit card. You'll have more luck getting reimbursed should your flight get cancelled. In addition, some credit cards give free flight and baggage insurance.

Finally, always remember to examine your ticket carefully. Check dates, flight times and numbers, and connecting cities for accuracy. Most important, copy down your ticket number and keep it separate from your ticket—having a record of your ticket number will make reimbursement easier if that ticket gets lost!

9.

Top Five Vacation
Ideas for Singles

It's never been easy for single travelers in the past. Hotel rates, excursion plans, even meal plans typically favor the couple or family. Lately, however, more options and discounts have been offered to the solo traveler, making it a commonplace practice.

So, where are today's singles headed on vacation? All over the world! From Thailand to Florida, single travelers are experiencing the joy of vacationing more than ever—sometimes in group situations, sometimes alone. Before booking, singles need to determine what type of experience they're looking for—a social atmosphere, an adventure holiday with outdoor recreational activities, or a relaxing getaway. Check out five of the most popular travel destinations for singles.

Group tours—Group travel tours are a great way to go if you're single. Travel companies like O Solo Mio, Singles Travel International, and Going Solo offer many, many trips for singles only—from outdoor adventure weekends to seven-day cruises. Best of all, these companies cater to singles exclusively—all ages—with special events and group sightseeing packages. Traveling this way removes the stress that many singles have over dining and lodging alone while away.

African safari—It's not for everyone, but the nature-loving, adventurous single traveler will revel in this magical atmosphere.

California wine country—Whether it's just to tour the vineyards of Napa, or cruise around San Francisco Bay, this popular vacation site offers everything from relaxation to outdoor nature hikes.

Spain—This hot spot has become a number-one locale for singles, with its excellent cuisine, beautiful sightseeing, and stunning, pristine beaches. There's nightlife on the Riviera and fabulous shopping in Madrid. From Spain, it's an easy trip to Morocco and that wonderfully romantic little place known as Casablanca.

Club Med—There are singles who swear by it. A Club Med vacation remains one of the most fun-in-the-sun places for anyone. All-inclusive, there's something to be said about not having to take out your wallet every five minutes. Club Med has it all—pools, beaches, and an amazing nightlife, chock-full of special themes and events. With no choice but to meet people, Club Med offers singles the best of what great vacations should offer!

10.

Top Five Vacation Ideas for Couples

For couples in love, the frustration of agreeing on the perfect romantic vacation can sometimes result in argument. Everybody has different interests, hobbies, and ideas of fun. So it's only natural that our vacation needs differ as well. Before you pick up the phone to book anything, sit down with your partner and make a list of three activities most important to each of you on vacation — even if one of those activities is "lying around on a chaise lounge with a frozen drink." This is the list to work from while planning your getaway. The destination you ultimately choose should have all six activities available.

What if you're looking at a list that includes both skiing and sunbathing? Sounds impossible, but it's really not. If your vacation is for a week or more, you can certainly find a place in the world to go where both skiing and sun-worshiping can be found: for example, California, Israel, Switzerland — just to name a few.

Childless couples looking for the perfect vacation are really the lucky bunch. They have a whole world of opportunities open to them

—no need to make any child-friendly adjustments. And they have the option of sharing expenses, as well as the best part—someone to travel with. Here are some favorite travel ideas for couples.

Sandals—Like Club Med for singles and families, Sandals is the place to go exclusively for couples. It offers an all-inclusive package, complete with nonstop, couples-only entertainment. But be aware: The majority of couples here are honeymooners.

Paris—With lower fares to the City of Lights, it's possible to visit gay Paris for just a weekend. Fine dining, superb museums, and some of the best accommodations in the world make up the formula for total romance. In fact, many Americans fly to Paris for the weekend to get engaged or married.

Bed and breakfast—A bed-and-breakfast weekend brings to mind an extravagant Victorian bedroom, a slew of fabulous antique shops, a roaring fire in a cozy living room, and home-cooked meals that comfort and dazzle your taste buds.

Cruising—Nothing brings a couple closer than spending a week on the high seas with a host of activities within walking distance from your cabin—if you decide to actually leave the cabin.

Camping—So many people shy away from vacationing in the great outdoors, but in fact, "roughing it" doesn't mean the same thing anymore. With sophisticated recreational vehicles equipped better than ever for camping, spending a few days in the middle of nowhere can be one of the most exhilarating vacations that a couple can take!

11.

Top Five Vacation Ideas for Families

Let's face it—when you have kids, vacations that include long, romantic walks along the beach and late-night dancing at the nearest margarita bar are over. Your vacation needs now include finding a hotel room that's child-protected and kid-friendly.

Family vacations are actually more fun than ever these days, with the majority of resorts and hotels catering exclusively to your children. Families are learning to get the most out of their time off together and enjoy lots of easy activities on vacation—in some cases at tremendously discounted savings.

Theme parks—Disney World is the number-one family vacation destination in the world. It can be one of the most fun-filled trips your family will ever spend together. Constant entertainment, full days of parades, rides, water parks, *and* fabulous hotels—with Disney, the possibilities are endless. With proper planning and tremendous organization, *any* theme park can be a fun and relaxing place to enjoy your family vacation.

Museums—If only the word "museum" didn't conjure up images in your child's mind of dull, boring hours spent looking at paintings. Unfortunately, it does. So why not replace "museum" with "theme park" the next time that you tell your kids where you're headed for vacation? With so many excellent, hands-on museums across the country, it would be terrible for your family to miss out on the experience. In New York City, go to the Natural History Museum *Theme Park*. In Washington, D.C., visit the Capital Children's Theme Park. The Center of Science & Industry *Theme Park* in Columbus, the Exploratorium in San Francisco, the Magic House in Missouri, the Please Touch *Theme Park* in Philadelphia—all are places worthy of building an entire family vacation around.

Travel abroad—How about your next family vacation in Scotland? Shuttling your entire clan across the globe for a vacation may sound like more trouble than it's worth, but in fact, many European destinations offer an enriching, educational, and exciting environment for the whole family. Scotland is just one—with its ancient historical sites, stunning scenery, stone-age homes, castles, islands, and *monsters* (Loch Ness), Scotland remains one of the most popular destinations abroad for families.

The beach—Everyone loves the beach! You don't even have to get on a plane to visit some of the world's best beaches. Bring your family to one of these top U.S. beach locations on your next vacation: Cape Cod, Charleston, Myrtle Beach, Hilton Head, the New Jersey Shore, the Hamptons of Long Island, San Diego, Palm

Beach, or Tampa. While you're at it, look into staying at a hotel chain like the Hyatt, which includes "camp" for kids at many of its locations. At night, while you and your spouse enjoy a romantic dinner for two, your kids will love the evening activities!

Suites — For the sweetest family vacation ever, no matter where you are headed, opt for a suite instead of a regular hotel room. Spread out in the extra space, cook breakfast in the nicely equipped kitchen, watch the news on one TV while the kids watch their favorite cartoons on another, and most important, close that bedroom door at night to give you and your spouse some much-needed privacy. After all, it's your vacation, too!

12.

Top Five Vacation
Ideas for Seniors

The sixty-five-and-over crowd has become such a major part of the traveling public that the travel industry continuously courts them with special discounts and deals. Seniors are usually flexible when it comes to travel dates and times, and they can take advantage of the least expensive deals to even the most desirable destinations.

Travel abroad is the most popular destination for seniors, in part because in many other countries of the world, older people are treated with far more honor and respect than they are in the United States. In addition, seniors and retirees take more extended vacations and have the time to engage in more activities while on vacation.

Elderhostels—With more than 10,000 offerings a year in more than one hundred countries, Elderhostel programs provide educational excellence, comfortable accommodations, delicious meals, and the warm camaraderie of fellow Elderhostel travelers.

Whether it's a two- to four-day trip to study the ecology of Puget Sound or a weeklong outdoor jaunt to Vermont to study the poetry of Robert Frost, there is an Elderhostel program to fit everyone's needs.

Cruises—Cruises are the most senior-friendly way to travel, offering the convenience of having everything—shopping, living, dining, recreational activities—right on board the ship, along with the option of visiting almost anywhere in the world.

Recreational vehicles (RVs)—More seniors are discovering the joys of RV life—in spacious, comfortable motor homes, sometimes lavishly decorated and equipped. This low-cost alternative to hotel lodging and airline or rail travel offers vacationers a great opportunity to see the world and make their own itinerary.

Spas and dude ranch resorts—Spas are among the most popular destinations for senior travelers. Not only do they offer therapeutic perks, they provide a host of activities in a rejuvenating atmosphere. The same goes for dude ranch resorts, which cater to large groups and gatherings. Offering individual or group activities such as horseback riding, water sports, and hiking, a dude ranch can be a great getaway for a large group of seniors traveling together. It's also the perfect place for a family reunion, with fun and games that allow Grandma and Grandpa to join in along with the grandkids.

Miami Beach, Florida—Maybe it's the constant sunshine, the early-bird specials, or the easy, breezy way of life, but for many seniors, this colorful Florida city has all they need for the perfect vacation.

No matter where you decide to go, if you're over fifty, it's a good idea to join the American Association of Retired Persons. This organization offers a travel service that designs tours and packages especially for senior travelers. With membership, you'll receive all kinds of discounts on airlines, hotels, and more.

13.

Big Plans,
Little Cash

You want to go away — you need to go away — but you're low on cash. Before you scratch your vacation plans, consider some low-cost options that might suit your pocket.

Sometimes, the exchange rate can actually be a deciding factor as to where to go! If Mexico, Venezuela, or Greece is giving a great rate on the American dollar, it might be a good idea to consider those countries as possible destinations for your vacation.

Before you leave on vacation, it also helps to establish a budget. Assign a portion of your budget for travel, a portion for lodging, a portion for food, and a portion for entertainment. Use your budget as a guide for negotiating even better prices. Then consider the money that you save as spending money for your trip. The key is to stick within whatever budget you have — no exceptions!

Ever dream of vacationing in a city such as New York, San Francisco, or Boston — and staying for free? It's possible — if you're agreeable to pet-sit! Check the classified ads in various cities looking for pet-sitters. In exchange for walking, feeding, and playing with Rover, you can get a great place to stay—free of charge.

Other options for inexpensive or rent-free lodging include house- or apartment-swapping. Again, your local classified section is the place to check for ads for apartments or homes available in other cities or countries. If you're flexible as to when you can travel, a swapping arrangement may be just the thing for you.

When it comes to airfare, you should never pay full price for a ticket. Be flexible and investigate the different tickets available and the restrictions placed upon them.

Looking to make the most of your hotel stay? Try asking for a free upgrade to the concierge floor once you arrive at the hotel. In a room at concierge level, you'll have access to free breakfasts and afternoon cocktails and snacks, thereby saving you money on food—especially if you're traveling with your family.

There are other ways to save while on vacation. Consider packing an extra bag full of snacks and instant breakfasts. A small electric immersion coil costs less than fifteen dollars and can give you the means for cooking in your hotel room at considerable savings. Take your cell phone and charger with you, should you plan on using the telephone. Your cell phone rate plan will always be lower for calls than the hotel's plan. One travel expert suggests investigating other long-distance services, like KALLBACK, that let you program their systems to call you. You won't have to pay excessive surcharges and taxes and the call is regarded as a free, incoming call.

When it comes to vacation spending, keep in mind that money saved in one portion of your budget, perhaps on airfare, might best be used in another area, like entertainment. Looking for ways to save every step of the way can really help you stretch your vacation budget further.

14.

Not-So-Frequent Fliers

An estimated 25 million Americans share some sort of fear of flying. Across the country, many airlines have begun to deal with the public's hesitance to fly. They even offer courses in combating fear of flying, complete with flight simulators and airline hostesses.

One way that the experts advise coping with a fear of flying is to develop an understanding of exactly what an airplane is doing throughout a flight. Having an idea of why every noise and every rattle occurs can help begin to ease flying fears.

There are some facts you should take into account if you are a hesitant flier. First of all, knowing that every aircraft can take off, fly, and land safely even if the engine fails should help ease your mind a bit. All pilots are trained for exactly that sort of thing. If turbulence causes you anxiety, it helps to know that the plane is, in fact, moving because of strong vertical air movements. An aircraft is designed to move quite roughly, even when faced with these strong forces. In fact, you'll be relieved to know that the plane has been put through tests much more severe than any turbulence can offer.

The noises heard, for the most part, during takeoff, include wing adjustments and wheel retraction. These noises can be loud, depending on the size of the aircraft and the location of your seat. As far as takeoff is concerned, most planes bank right after taking off, most likely in the direction of the flight. Descent and landing have similar noises—as the wheels lock into place and the wing flaps assume their landing configuration.

Since knowledge is by far the best way to combat fear of flying, take it one step further and really get into your flight! See if you can tell which states or countries you're flying over. Try to distinguish the different types of clouds outside your window. Some international flights post the plane's altitude and route on a screen during the flight. Many people find that knowing where they are and how high they're flying helps ease their anxiety.

Simple ways to ease the stress of flying include sitting toward the front of the plane—where the ride will be smoother and quieter—and in an aisle seat, if looking out the window scares you. If all else fails, ask your doctor to prescribe a mild muscle relaxant and take it an hour before takeoff. While this really works best, keep in mind that it could backfire if your flight is delayed, or it may present a problem if you're traveling with children.

Whatever you do, don't drink alcohol to ease your fears. You could wind up both scared *and* sick to your stomach!

15.

Arriving Stress-Free

There's no question that travel—whether by plane, train, or automobile—can be an uncomfortable, unpleasant experience. Cramped seating, inadequate legroom, cabin pressure, noisy children—there are a host of factors involved that can make the entire experience aggravating.

Despite what you're up against, there are certain measures that you can take to ensure you arrive at your travel destination relaxed, composed, and ready to begin your vacation. A few simple, airline-approved and recommended exercises can be done in your seat with your seat belt fastened. These exercises help to stimulate circulation and stretch and relax cramped muscles.

During extended car or plane trips, it's your neck that's most at risk of muscle tension. It's important to keep your jaw muscles as loose as possible, as they directly affect your neck. (If you're a nervous flier, try not to clench your teeth during the flight.) To loosen neck muscles, lean your head as far forward as possible to feel the stretch down the back of your neck. Try it for twenty seconds. Then lean your head to the right for twenty seconds, then to the left, feeling the stretch down the sides of your neck. Next, let your head drop back while arching your upper back.

Shoulder rolls can also do wonders to relieve neck and back tension. Roll them forward simultaneously, then back, then forward again, this time alternating right and left, then back, right and left.

If your seat has armrests, you can use them to help stretch out your lower back—a major sore spot during travel. Grab the back of your left armrest with your right hand and twist your upper body around to look behind you. If you're in the minivan, smile at your kids for twenty seconds or so and then turn back and twist to the other side. If you're on a plane, you can smile at the people behind you. Who knows? You may make some new friends.

Get your arms and legs moving, too, to prevent circulation problems and cramps. With one arm at a time, reach up (in the car, you may have to reach up and over) and then relax, ten times with each arm. To help ease tension in your legs, lift one thigh off your seat to raise your foot from the floor, then rotate your foot in each direction. Repeat with the other foot.

These simple exercises should help with the muscle tension and cramping associated with long-trip travel. Of course, it goes without saying that if you're driving, you should make frequent stops—even if it's just to walk around in circles for a few minutes or let your kids run wild. If you're flying, it helps immensely to get up and move around the cabin whenever possible.

As for the stress brought on by noisy children? There's relatively little that you can do about that. Investigate investing in a portable DVD player and stock up on some kid flicks for the trip.

16.

Airplane Kiddie Bag

Until your airplane seat has been kicked in the back by a child for the umpteenth time during the course of a transatlantic flight, you may not be able to comprehend exactly how irritating it actually is. Sure, you're most likely more concerned about tending to the needs of your children on the airplane, but there's nothing more stressful than being on the receiving end of a constant barrage of glares and comments from victimized passengers! With that in mind, your sole mission before undergoing an airplane trip should be to keep your kids entertained and account for their every minute of the flight.

Your first order of business should be to prepare your kids for what to expect on an airplane days before you leave. Read them books about airplane trips, talk to them about manners and airplane etiquette, and above all, ask them what they would like to bring on the plane to keep busy. Then bring twice as much.

Each traveling child should have his or her very own carry-on—a backpack that opens and closes easily, with lots of pockets for lots of stuff. For children three and older, bring activity books, a pack of crayons (skip the markers), a pad of plain white paper, tons of stickers, small toys such as little figurines, toy cars, small storybooks or travel games, and puzzles. Though you may prefer your older children to read or participate in some other mind-stimulating activity on the flight, this is actually the perfect time to let them play their handheld electronic games to their hearts' content. Make them aware, however, that the pilot may require all electronic items be turned off during takeoff and landing.

Traveling with babies is a whole other ball game. Leave prepared for a *normal* outing with the baby, then toss in extra of everything in case of delays or to tide you over for the first twenty-four hours of your trip. It may be that long until you arrive, claim your bags, find a taxi, and get to the hotel. Airlines will provide baby food, but chances are that it isn't the same food your baby is used to. Though they may weigh down your diaper bag considerably, pack small jars of your baby's favorites, along with your own supply of milk, juice, fruit, crackers, Cheerios, and so on.

Extra snacks in general are essential for kids of all ages, since once you're up in the air, it's usually limited to peanuts and crackers. Pack your children's favorites, along with an extra juice box or two of the juice they prefer. And don't forget the bubble gum—let them chew during takeoff and landing to equalize the pressure behind their eardrums. Let your baby nurse or drink during these times to relieve his or her ear pressure. Above all, keep reminding your children about seat-kicking!

17.

Travel Safety

Understanding the risks involved with any type of travel has been an important issue for decades, but only recently has air travel become so closely monitored. Before this time of heightened security, the risk that you took most often when traveling was having your wallet stolen.

Having your valuables stolen while on vacation is still a much more common risk than having your plane hijacked. Travelers should take the possibility of being robbed very seriously on vacation—no matter where they're traveling to. Even the most prestigious hotels have room safes. One can infer from this that hotels have little control over their staff or neighborhood incidents. It's probably a better idea to travel light—no matter where you're going—and leave your precious possessions and valuables back at home in your safety deposit box.

There are some valuables you simply must travel with—including your passport, air tickets, money, traveler's checks, and credit cards. Your best bet is to keep these items with you at all times—preferably in a money belt worn under your clothes.

Thieves often work areas heavy with tourists: at outdoor events, shopping areas, bus stations, and airports. Pickpockets prey upon unsuspecting men who keep their wallets in their hip or back pockets and naïve women who carry dangling handbags.

Wearing a money belt can prevent this—pickpockets can't get to your money if it's strapped and secured to your body, under your clothes. It may take some getting used to, but rest assured, it'll be worth not worrying about getting ripped off.

Women travelers—especially those traveling alone—are at a particularly big disadvantage when it comes to travel safety. A lack of understanding different cultures may make you vulnerable. Returning to your hotel late at night presents a safety issue for single women, as does getting a room at the far end of a long hallway. Reject an isolated room or a room that's located next to a stairway or on the ground floor. Avoid searching for your key in an empty hallway. Be curt with male hotel staff to avoid anything that may be perceived as an invitation to the very people who have access to your room. Above all, never get on an elevator alone with anyone who makes you feel uncomfortable. Trust your intuition.

Travel safety involves, for the most part, common sense. Whether you're part of a couple, part of a family, or traveling alone; boarding a plane or checking into a hotel room; shopping in a bazaar or having dinner in town; use your head and trust your instincts. If something or someone makes you uncomfortable, chances are that your feelings are on the mark. Don't ever worry about being rude — just remove yourself from the situation and head for a safer environment.

18.

What to Pack?

Pack light. That's the general rule of thumb, no matter where you're headed. In fact, travel experts advise you to take half the clothes that you think you'd need on vacation—and twice the money.

Travelers are all the same. No matter where we're headed, we always think that the weather and the situation will be similar to where we're leaving from. So all those "just in case" clothes, like the raincoat or jacket when you're going to a tropical island, just leads to overpacking. Think honestly about it: What are you going to be doing all day and how often will you really change your clothes?

Once on your trip, the weight of your bag becomes much more of a concern to you than the actual items that you've brought. If you can carry your case around comfortably, then you're ready to roll. If not, something must go!

Don't buy a whole new wardrobe for your trip. Take your favorite, comfortable clothes that you know look good on you. Layer cotton T-shirts and lightweight sweaters for evenings and colder climates, and bring a windbreaker for warmer climates. Men may want to bring along a sports jacket, especially if you plan on dining out on your trip. Make sure that whatever you bring can be hand-washed, or check on the reliability of the dry-cleaning service at your hotel.

Take comfortable shoes. Even your dressy shoes should be worn-in and comfy. You'll need just one pair of your best walking shoes or sneakers—in addition to the pair that you're wearing to the airport—and that's it.

Before you leave, weigh your bag! Twenty pounds is plenty. If you're tipping the scale over twenty, choose five things to leave at home!

19.

Choosing the
Perfect Paperback

If you polled most Americans as to when they last read a book, the majority would reply, "While on vacation." Millions of people each year swarm the bookstores and libraries at vacation time (Christmas and spring and summer breaks) in the hopes of finding the perfect book to complement their vacation.

Reading a book on vacation has many benefits. The first is entertainment—especially during a long flight or car ride, or on a rainy vacation day. But a bigger benefit to reading while on vacation is the relaxation factor. When you settle down with a good book, your heart rate mellows, your muscles relax, and the only thing that's being taxed is your imagination! Make sure that you bring a book along on your next vacation—even if you're planning on full days of sightseeing or physical activity. You'll be surprised at what a welcome, calming effect the act of reading will have.

Choosing the perfect vacation paperback is an important part of preparing for your trip. You need to choose wisely, especially if this is one of the only times that you get the opportunity to read. Make sure that you get a book that will last you the duration of your trip. Just remember that a super-long book or a brand-new hardcover is going to be *heavy*.

20.

Ten Things to Pack
for Stress-Free Travel

There's nothing worse than the unexpected while on vacation. You've planned and organized for your vacation for months and when something happens that affects your plans, you're understandably upset. But there are ways to avoid small problems that are bound to arise. Consider the following items when packing for your trip, and bring some or all of them along with you.

Plastic bags are a traveler's friend. Consider bringing five plastic trash bags (kitchen size) with you for dirty laundry, wet clothes, and so on, and a few plastic zipper bags as well. They are extremely convenient for toting snacks and just about everything else. It's also a good idea to pack all your shampoo bottles and toiletries in zipper bags before putting them in your suitcase to protect your things from spills or leaks.

Liquid soap and stain-remover wipes are great for hand-washing clothes and getting stains or spills out of most everything. Moist towelettes or facial wipes are perfect for travel. Slip a good amount into your suitcase. If you're traveling with children, double the amount.

Hopefully you won't need these, but copies of your passport, driver's license, traveler's check numbers, and credit cards may come in handy. Pack the copies, and leave them hidden in your suitcase.

A sewing kit can mend accidental rips, tears, or lost buttons. For traveling abroad, you may also need an adapter. Many hotels abroad offer hair dryers and irons in the room, but you may have other electronics that need to be charged (a cell phone or video camera battery, for example). An eyeglasses repair kit if you wear them (or sunglasses) will come in handy if you'd be lost without them.

Antibacterial cream or ointment or any all-in-one pharmaceutical product that can aid insect bites, minor cuts, and burns, and moisturize severely dry skin can save room when packing toiletries.

Finally, a money belt is the best way to avoid disastrous vacation situations. Each person (children included) should wear his or her own money belt.

21.

Don't Pack the
Whole Medicine Cabinet

If you have children and you're planning a vacation, your children will inevitably get sick either the night before or on the first day of your vacation. But major illness aside, you'll be glad to learn that you can still go ahead with your vacation plans even when someone in your traveling party becomes sick. If there's no time to make a quick trip to the doctor, find a doctor who will take pity on you and write you a prescription for an antibiotic to bring along, just in case. It's also a great idea to call your insurance company before you leave on vacation to learn what medications are covered, and where you can go to get them while you're away, should you or a family member fall ill.

There are, however, ways of cutting down the amount of remedies you bring with you. The first trick helps size down the first-aid load quite considerably: Purchase small, travel-size bottles and choose tablets and caplets over liquid medicines.

Use a small cosmetics bag or a plastic box to construct your vacation first-aid kit. (Bags work best because they can be crammed into a suitcase.) Inside, pack the following items: adhesive bandages; topical antibacterial cream; moisturizer with aloe; sunburn relief cream; moleskin (for blisters); individually wrapped antiseptic towelettes; insect repellent; sunscreen; a thermometer (in a hard case); tweezers; an analgesic; ten to fifteen each of ibuprofen caplets, acetaminophen caplets, and allergy pills; a small bottle of children's ibuprofen (or dissolvable tablets, if they're old enough to take them); a small bottle (or dissolvable tablets) of children's acetaminophen and a measuring cup; antimalarial pills; seasickness pills; and last, but not least, antidiarrheal for adults and children.

Sound like a lot? It is! But it's better to be prepared than to have to find these remedies in a foreign country's drugstore. Many places don't carry the same brand names or the same medications. So find a way to stuff in all of these potentially necessary items.

22.

How to Leave Your House

Once you've scheduled, packed, and confirmed, you'll realize that the most important thing about leaving for vacation has yet to be done: securing your home so it will be safe while you're away. Don't let your empty house become a target for every burglar and thief. Take the necessary precautions to secure it properly so that you'll have peace of mind while you're away.

Start by finding somebody (a neighbor, a close relative, or a baby-sitter) to check on your house every day. This includes making sure the family pet is fed, the mail is brought in, and your plants are watered. Remember to leave this person a copy of your travel itinerary with a list of telephone numbers where you can be reached. You may also want to leave a copy of your passport and flight information. The fewer people who know that you're away, the better.

Your second move should be to suspend all deliveries—newspapers, bottled water, milk—you don't want things accumulating on your front porch indicating that you are not at home. If no one is available to help you, the post office can hold your mail for you until you return. Other surefire ways of letting a burglar know that your house is empty are letting your lawn grow too high, or leaving ten inches of snow on your second car and driveway. Prepay your gardener to cut your grass. If it's winter, prepay someone to handle all snow removal.

Once the car is packed and you're ready to leave, it's time to do a final house security check. Make sure that all your doors and windows are locked—especially if they are on the ground floor. Also make sure that your curtains are closed.

An automatic timer for your lights can keep commonly used rooms upstairs and downstairs well lit at night. One of those rooms should be a bathroom, since that's a room that could conceivably be used day and night.

If you have a security system, you may want to let the service know that you'll be away. If you don't have a security system, buy some fake alarm company stickers and fix them to your windows by the front door.

Finally, unplug small appliances and turn your heat or air conditioning to an average level lower than you live with. Leave for your trip with a clear head and minimal anxiety. And remember to empty your garbage before you go—or you'll come home to a less than pleasant odor!

23.

Did I Leave
the Oven On?

The gnawing, nagging feeling that you've forgotten something after locking up your home and leaving for vacation is one shared by millions of travelers. There's nothing more aggravating than realizing that you forgot to leave a key for the neighbor at the same time that you're pulling into the airport.

Your first order of business before leaving for vacation is to mark a warning flag on your home calendar exactly two days before you're scheduled to travel. Make a list of everything that you can think of that you'll need while you're away. Make a separate checklist of things to do before leaving the house.

Next, begin to prepare a "document bag." It should include items such as your passport, visa, copy of birth certificate, driver's license, airplane tickets, certificate of vaccination, extra passport photos, membership cards for organizations that you belong to (like AAA or the AARP), basic medical information with your physician's name and number, the phone number of whomever is watching your home, and your prescription medicines. Organize these items neatly in your document bag, and then hide it in the trunk of the car that you plan to take to the airport.

Tape your to-do checklist to whichever door you usually leave your house from. This way, you'll be sure to remember all of those easily forgettable things, like unplugging all electrical appliances, closing and locking all windows and doors, giving your neighbor the house key and your itinerary, taking out the garbage, and, of course, making sure that the oven is off.

24.

Leaving the
Kids Behind

Leaving the kids behind and jetting off for a romantic vacation with your spouse is supposed to be relaxing and exhilarating. Yet for many couples, the mere planning and organizing for the few days that they'll be apart from their kids can be so stressful that going on vacation becomes counterproductive!

What all vacation-bound parents must understand is that their children can survive without them for a few days. In fact, it can even be beneficial for children to spend short periods of time away from their parents while being supervised by other mature, capable adults. It gives the children an opportunity to relate to adults other than their parents teaches them behavior and manners outside the family, and for children who are left with grandparents, gives them the chance to form a special bond without interference from Mom and Dad.

One way for parents to cut the stress associated with leaving their children for an extended period of time is to prepare an itinerary and information packet for the caregivers as early as possible. Many parents overburdened with packing and planning for their trip leave this important job for the last minute and then find themselves scribbling instructions haphazardly and leaving important information out.

Begin by charting your children's daily schedules in an organized manner on separate sheets of paper. Remember to include all of their activities—with starting and ending times—chores, homework, and play dates. Instruct their caregiver as to how much time is needed to travel to certain activities, and provide emergency phone numbers if carpooling is involved.

A few days before leaving for vacation, make a list of your children's important information: doctors' numbers, medicine dosages, teachers' names, emergency contacts, meals that they prefer, and basic medical history. Keep this list near your bed at night, with a pen close by, so that you can jot down important items when you think of them. On the night before your departure, you should begin organizing that list in a better fashion, making sure it's legible.

When your vacation day arrives, don't panic! Make sure to leave time for a hugging and kissing session—one that is long enough to ease the separation anxiety...*yours!*

25.

Party of
Twenty-Seven

The problem with vacationing in large groups is that the more people you have, the more opinions you'll need to contend with. This problem usually presents itself at mealtimes, when discussion and debate over where and what to eat can take longer than the meal itself. Differences in opinions in other areas as well—where to go, what to see, how to get there, and how long to stay—can also result in some not-so-friendly tension, even among the best of friends.

The best advice, should you be contemplating a vacation with friends or joining a group of families for an extended trip, is to look for a preplanned vacation or group tour. This immediately removes the decision-making process from your itinerary, since all activities and meals are preplanned, organized, and led by a tour guide.

Another way to avoid the complications of group travel is to debate and make your decisions before you depart on your trip. At home, in a relaxed atmosphere, you can all plan the entire trip, discussing which activities best suit your group and what meals or restaurants would be appropriate. It may take a little fun out of being flexible and spontaneous, but it sure beats standing around on a street corner with a party of twenty-seven, debating the pros and cons of some restaurant someone has heard about. Remember, too, to include a day or so in your plans for some alone time, especially if you're planning to be away with the group for more than a few days. Even the best of friends can get on each other's nerves after a couple of days of doing everything together.

Most important, choose your travel companions wisely. Personalities don't magically change while on vacation, so think carefully about whom you commit to travel with. If you have children, make sure that they'll have travel mates around the same age and sex, and that you've included activities that they can all enjoy.

26.

No Children Allowed

As unbelievable as it seems, there are many parents who insist on bringing their young children to places that specifically advise against it. Sometimes, obviously, parents don't have a choice but to bring their young children along to certain places, and that's understandable. But other times, when a baby-sitter or a cancellation of plans would be deemed more appropriate, it's a wonder why they don't heed the warnings of "Not Intended for Young Children." That warning is there for a reason—usually being that the subject matter, or perhaps the atmosphere of a certain place, is decidedly too mature for little ones.

Parents should absolutely expose their children to culture, theater, fine art, and even fine dining, but at an appropriate age. They need to remember that shop owners, museum directors, and theater lobbies prohibit children for a reason. Parents balk at signs on museum or restaurant doors that say, "Children Not Permitted," figuring that they should be the ones to decide whether some subject matter is appropriate or not for their kids.

That said, if you're a parent, the next time that you plan your vacation, put your children's interests first. If you anticipate visiting places for mature audiences, consider staying at a hotel that is known for its childcare and children's activities. This way, you can set some time aside to visit those places while your children are entertained and cared for.

Dragging your toddler to something that you know is too mature —just to satisfy your own vacation needs—is asking for trouble. You'll find yourself contending with a disagreeable, unhappy child, not to mention the angry stares of other adults who have left their own children home with baby-sitters.

27.

Airports 101

Airports remain one of the most confusing, aggravating, frustrating, and potentially infuriating places that we must visit in life. But flying is a part of many of our vacations, so it helps to read up as much as possible on the inner workings of the particular airports on your itinerary and prepare yourself for the worst-case scenarios. Remember to devise a backup plan, should all else fail.

Before backing out of your driveway en route to the airport, call the airport and check on your flight. One prominent travel expert advises to take this even one step further and ask the phone attendant for something known as the "FLIFO" (internal flight information) number when you call. Once you're given your FLIFO aircraft number, then you should ask the status of that number. This, in fact, will give you the *true* status of your flight.

Be sure to understand your airline's security policy before going to the airport, and ask for tips on how to make the experience run more smoothly. Next, find someone to take you to the airport rather than driving yourself. Gridlock at the airport during morning or evening rush hour can result in you missing your departure completely. If you're dropped off at the departures level instead, you can almost always go right in.

If you can't cram all of your vacation items into your two allotted carry-on bags, and you're vacationing with others, remember that every traveler—including children and babies—has the same baggage allowance as you. If you're a family of four, your best bet would be to pack all of your vacation belongings into eight smaller bags and carry them all onto the plane. This way, you won't need to check anything.

You may also want to consider sending one large suitcase to your hotel by overnight delivery. It may cost a little more, but it may save you the time and trouble of checking your bag and having to wait for it at baggage claim. In addition, you'll avoid the possibility of the airline losing your bags.

One of the most important things that you should make yourself aware of is airport crime. Airport criminals prey upon foreigners, and every traveler is at risk. Most airport criminals—pickpockets and scam artists, in particular—work in pairs, targeting solo travelers most often. Avoid being robbed at an airport by being alert at all times. Don't fall for their professional methods of distracting you— make sure to have a firm hold on your belongings at all times. Travel experts warn against putting your bags down while talking on the phone, or leaving them alone at all.

Your last order of business before boarding is to recheck the status of your flight. If it's on time, head straight for the gate. Always try to be among the first on the plane if you can — this way, you're guaranteed some overhead space for your carry-on luggage and your share of pillows and blankets!

28.

Car Rental Reality

Renting a car seems harmless enough, but in fact there are quite a few key things that consumers need to know to ensure that they don't get taken for a ride! One lesser-known "trick" to getting a good deal, for instance, is to reserve a car at the weekly rate instead of a daily rate. This is especially important if you're not sure when you'll be returning the car. When in doubt, reserve it for longer than you'll need. You'll never be charged extra for returning it early, but you can be sure that there's a hefty charge for returning it late!

There are other factors that can add substantial fees to your car rental bill. When renting an automobile, it helps to ask about all the extra charges, fees, and taxes associated with the rental, thus eliminating any surprises when it comes time to pay.

Reserving your rental car online can be not only cheaper but faster than calling the company's 800 number or standing in line at the airport. Reserve at least a week in advance if you can, in order to get the best deal.

Be aware of drop-off charges! Most rental companies will charge you more for returning your car to a destination other than the one from which you picked it up. Some companies offer special deals for one-way trips, but such deals may be limited to certain parts of the country.

Avoid the added anxiety of liability (should you get into an accident in your rental car), and read up on your personal insurance plan. It may cover you in the event of an accident, so you may not need to purchase costly insurance through the rental company.

Finally, save even more time by making sure that you have the proper documents at pickup time. Most rental companies require that you have a credit card in the same name as your valid driver's license in order to rent. Most companies, too, require you to be at least twenty-five years old. When you pick up your rental car, inspect the vehicle for damages before driving off!

Last tip: Ask for an extra key. You wouldn't believe how many people lock themselves out of rental cars while on vacation—just stopping for a second at an overlook to enjoy the view!

29.

Surviving the
Family Road Trip

A family car trip has to be meticulously planned solely around the comfort of the children. For example, if you want your children to sleep, make sure that you bring a pillow and small blanket along for each of them. Leave very early in the morning, perhaps even taking them straight out of bed to the car, still in their pajamas.

A well-stocked automobile can make the difference between a great family road trip and a disastrous one. Pack a cooler for the trip, but be sure to include a regular meal and water or milk, rather than snacks and sugary drinks. This way, the first rest stop can take place a few hours after departure, when everyone is ready for a meal, a stretch, and a chance to use the bathrooms.

Have your children put together their own entertainment packs for the ride, with activity books, crayons, lightweight car games, a "lap desk" pillow, books, and CDs or cassettes. Remember that if they plan to bring video games, they will need light attachments if you plan to be in the car after dark. An "over-the-seat" car pack, hung on the back of both the driver's seat and the front passenger's seat, can hold even more fun things for the kids.

The rule of thumb for car travel is to stop every hour and a half to two hours to give everyone a chance to move around or use the bathroom. Parents need to anticipate fatigue and hunger during any lengthy car trip.

Finally, it is extremely important for both parents to memorize the trip route before leaving home! For car trips, maps should only be used in case of highway closings, to look up alternate routes of travel.

30.

When Nature Calls

For many, the thought of "roughing it" on a camping trip in the middle of the woods, with no running water, electricity, or bathroom facilities, is a complete turnoff. Camping trips conjure up images of Boy or Girl Scouts trying to light a campfire by rubbing two sticks together, or sleepless nights of swatting at flies in a cold, cramped tent.

But those of us who have actually camped out during the past ten years have become privy to the best-kept secret in the world of travel: Camping can be a luxurious, tremendously fun, and inexpensive way to see the world!

Campgrounds all over the world are suddenly being booked up far in advance. Camping is convenient, scenic, and much cheaper than a hotel. Vacationers around the globe are learning the joys of camping and going back to nature for their vacation fun.

Camping gear has certainly changed over the years, making camping trips easier for vacationers. The double-flap tents preferred by scouts have long ago been transformed into five-room tents with living room and dining areas! They can be set up in a snap, folded away in minutes, and in some cases, can be adjusted for standing room. Tents are now constructed from a resilient, thermal material that's all-weather friendly. Sleeping bags, cookout gear, and battery-operated everything have also made "roughing it" a lot less rough! Portable lamps, toilets, showers, refrigerators, and mattresses—all of which can be packed to fit in or on a regular family-size automobile—have certainly made it a lot easier for modern folk to go *au natural*.

Recreational vehicles have also gone through major changes over the years. Some are lavishly equipped with running water, shower and kitchen facilities, and beautiful living space. RVs have become the only way that millions of Americans will travel.

Camping is as popular in Europe as it is in the United States. Just make sure to reserve your space ahead of time, because like the best hotels, the best campgrounds often fill up during peak times.

31.

The Perfect Family Vacation

A "perfect" getaway means different things to different families. Some families consider their vacation successful if they've all returned still on speaking terms. Other families deem their trip perfect if they've seen every single attraction on their sightseeing checklist. Still others feel that they've had a great vacation if no family member broke a limb or needed an antibiotic.

The most important element of the "perfect" family vacation, however, is the destination. It must be so special, so right for the family, that both parents and kids can't stop talking about it.

Do these destinations exist? They sure do! In the United States, there are fabulous family-friendly spots in every corner, every state, and along every coast. A recent poll among 2,500 parents revealed the top family vacation destinations in the country. Of those results, one stood out more than others—a vacation that includes scenery, clear water, tons of sunshine, desert canyons, and hundreds of sandy beaches: houseboating!

Yes, houseboating has again become a popular family recreational choice, with all the comforts of home, lots of privacy, and very easy access to water fun! Combined with another top pick for the perfect family destination—southern Utah's Lake Powell—it's a top-notch vacation match made in heaven.

Other top destinations included Walt Disney World; Yellowstone National Park; Washington, D.C.; Mount Rushmore; Sea World Orlando; Yosemite National Park; the San Diego Zoo; Chicago's Museum of Science and Industry; the Magic House in Missouri, the Indianapolis Children's Museum; the Grand Canyon; the Statue of Liberty; and Niagara Falls.

Whichever destination you choose and whichever corner of the world you choose to explore with your family, there is one thing to bear in mind. Keeping your kids safe, healthy, and happy while traveling is what really makes for the "perfect" family vacation.

32.

Traveling Alone

Traveling alone can open you to unique personal experiences in new places. Solo travelers should take full advantage of these opportunities—while still maintaining their safety.

While on vacation, search for that comfort level that you have on your own at home by following the same routines: Drink a cup of coffee in the morning or take an afternoon jog. When you head out to a restaurant, bring a book, your journal, or materials for writing letters and postcards, or use the quiet time to plan the next part of your trip.

Visit one shop consistently or have breakfast at the same café each morning, and get to know the people who work there. They will be able to offer you advice and suggestions about the area that you are visiting.

By far, the most important aspect of traveling alone is practicing personal safety. Consider learning basic self-defense. Research your destination so that you'll know what to expect in terms of attitudes toward foreigners, and if you're female, toward women. If you're a solo female traveler, you should never be apologetic or feel that you're being rude by telling someone with whom you're uncomfortable to leave you alone.

For your hotel stay, request a room that isn't on the ground floor, which can offer easy access through a window. Avoid opening your door to people who are unknown to you or who do not identify themselves. Become familiar with the people at your hotel's reception desk, and inform them of your comings and goings. It helps to blend in by dressing like a local resident, or at least by trying to look inconspicuous in your dress and behavior. Walk with confidence, and avoid standing clueless on a street corner, poring over a map!

Above all, enjoy yourself! Think about how lucky you are to be traveling alone and making your own decisions about what to do, where to go, and when to eat or sleep. You'll have more interaction with local people and more opportunity to meet other travelers than do couples or families traveling together.

33.

The Importance
of Being Prepared

Certain documents that are required for travel abroad must be applied for and acquired some months in advance of your vacation. Passports, for example, require application three months in advance, and you have to apply in person. If you already have a passport, check to make sure that it doesn't expire until well after you return home. You'll need to apply for a new passport if it stands to expire within two months of your return, if it was issued more than twelve years ago, if you were under eighteen when it was first issued, or if you've legally changed your name. A renewal can be done by mail or in person.

It is a good idea to register your passport at the U.S. embassy when you arrive in a foreign country. This can expedite getting it replaced, should it become lost or stolen. Passport theft abroad is a common occurrence, as the black market for fake passports is huge. Should your passport get lost or stolen, it also helps to have a copy of your birth certificate, previous passport, driver's license or ID, and extra passport photos. Keep your passport *on your person* for your entire trip.

You'll need to secure a visa in order to visit some countries. A visa is an endorsement of entry into another country, proof that your papers and intended purpose of travel are acceptable to that government. Most travelers are never sure if they'll need a visa for the country that they'll be visiting. Most Americans don't need a visa to visit another country, unless travel to that country is restricted, as it is to Cuba. Your best bet is to consult your travel agent, the consulate, or the embassy. The airline or tour package operator should also know. Most European countries do not require American citizens to have visas—they assume that we're going to want to return to America—but other countries have different requirements, so it's a good idea to check.

If you're looking to drive a car while abroad, you may also want to obtain an international driver's permit. In Europe, the only country where it's required is Spain. Elsewhere, your regular state driver's license is sufficient. Outside Europe, many countries require an international permit. Check with AAA or your local automobile club for information on obtaining one. The more that you take care of early in preparation for your trip, the less stress you'll be likely to encounter!

34.

Traveling on the Fly

Last-minute, spontaneous, "pack-your-bags-we're-leaving-now!" trips can be some of the most exciting vacations you'll ever have. And when you make travel plans at the last minute, you may be eligible for less expensive airfares and hotel rooms. As any travel expert will tell you, the airlines and hotels would much rather sell you their empty seats or rooms for whatever they can get than leave those seats and rooms empty.

The benefits of last-minute traveling can be truly inspiring! Last-minute vacations offer the perfect opportunity to reenergize yourself and your relationships, and prepare you to face the future with renewed motivation.

When should you just leave it all behind and jet off to distant shores? Some great escape times include the weekend after a particularly cumbersome project or deal at work, right after a major holiday that you've hosted at home, after you've planned a big event like a wedding, or even just before your own wedding! Refuel your mind and body, and enjoy all the perks that come with just "taking off"!

35.

All-Inclusive, or All-Intrusive?

For many people, an all-inclusive trip is the perfect vacation solution. You pay for everything in advance—the airfare, hotel room, meals, drinks, activities, and entertainment—and then spend the entire vacation free of money concerns (with the exception of tipping).

Travelers on a tight budget should definitely look into an all-inclusive vacation package. More often than not, thrifty travelers budget their vacation and then forget to include the "extras" that they spend *during* the vacation. With an all-inclusive, that's never a concern.

Parents with kids in tow can still have a romantic vacation at an all-inclusive resort—provided that they choose one with great children's programs. Kids will enjoy participating in age-appropriate activities, making new friends, and quite possibly learning about a new culture, while their folks can get a massage, enjoy a quiet meal together, or catch up on downtime.

Some all-inclusive resorts cater exclusively to honeymooners. Vacations have recently become a popular form of wedding gift, offering wedding guests or the parents of the bride and groom an opportunity to make the couple's postnuptial trip a gift. It's even possible for the bride and groom to register for an all-inclusive vacation.

If you're thinking about getting married, several all-inclusive resorts offer free weddings! Experienced wedding planners work at the resorts and take care of all the details, down to simplifying the proper paperwork and marriage licenses.

Should you decide to vacation all-inclusively, the most important thing that you need to do is make sure you are headed to a resort with activities geared toward *your* enjoyment. There are all-inclusive resorts for every type of traveler, whether you're looking for sports, nightlife, or fine dining.

36.

Cruise Control

Rock climb in the morning, ice skate after lunch, catch a magic show after dinner, and then gamble until dawn. Or soak up the sun, scuba dive, then stroll through the European city of your choice. It's all possible to do in a day—on a cruise ship! When it comes to cruising vacations, options range from trips to exotic Asia to sailing the seas with Mickey Mouse!

Every ship has a personality, and some cruise lines specialize in specific traits. Some cater especially to kids and families, others to water sports fanatics, and still others to travelers who want to sightsee and experience fine cuisine.

A cruise promises its passengers a week of total escape. However, all that peace and quiet will cost you. Most cruises are all-inclusive (meals and activities on board are usually included), but bring a lot of small bills for tipping. If it is in your budget, the excitement of activities and learning experiences to choose from, never having to hear the words "I'm bored!" and the simple unadulterated fun that a cruising vacation offers are priceless anyway!

37.

Unconventional Vacations

For many, lazing around poolside, sipping iced drinks with miniature umbrellas is not their idea of a vacation. In their attempt to escape the monotony of everyday life, these travelers instead seek heart-pumping, adrenaline-surging adventure!

At the bookstore, you'll find many guides to great outdoor adventures, from heli-skiing (being dropped off atop a snowy mountain by helicopter and skiing down a path with no trail) to whitewater rafting. You'll also find sites online that cater to adventure travel. You'll find information on places to go for the best climbing, cycling, diving, fly-fishing, camping, mountain biking, and surfing, to name a few. These sites have tips for beginners and bulletin boards filled with ideas from other travelers. If you're new to adventure vacationing, ask your travel agent to suggest some companies specializing in the kind of vacation that you're looking for.

You have to be fit to be an adventure traveler, but if you book your trip far enough in advance, you can train for it in the months before. Safety is a huge consideration in this high-risk area of recreation, so be sure to weigh all travel risks and take necessary precautions before you book your trip. Heed the U.S. State Department travel warnings if you're headed to a foreign country, and examine the health conditions and political disturbances of that region. Prepare yourself, as well, for personal health emergencies. Investigate where to find reliable health care fast, and what facilities are available to you. Keep your medical information on a laminated card in your wallet, including your physician's name and phone number.

Adventure travel can be fascinating and exhilarating. But you may need a vacation from your vacation when you return!

38.
Surviving
Theme Parks

Theme parks are not for everyone, but at one time or another, everyone will eventually find themselves visiting one. You had better learn now how to survive.

Your first course of action before you even agree to go to a specific park is to get yourself a map of the park. Have it mailed to you ahead of time, if possible. The map is the key to navigating the park and reducing the inevitable stress that comes from staring at poorly labeled signs and wasting precious time. Learning the park's layout ahead of time can protect you and your loved ones from getting lost or separated. You'll be able to better plan your day, making sure not to log more miles than needed while carrying little ones or pushing a stroller!

Theme park visits don't have to be stressful. As with any other vacation, you just need to prepare yourself for the frustrations that present themselves and avoid them. Waiting on line can be avoided with a little advance knowledge of the inner workings of the attraction times and schedules. You can turn a long line into a breakfast picnic and character visit! Make a game of map-reading with the kids to help minimize their theme park hysteria, which often happens when parents can't move as fast through a park as their kids.

Your theme park day pack needs to be carefully planned as well. You'll need a cooler section for prepared lunches and water, antibacterial wipes for messes, adhesive bandages, a towel for water rides, a dry space to keep your maps, money, and tickets, and small activity books or toys for line-waiting. Each adult should carry one day pack.

Finally, forget about how old your kids are: Spend the money on a stroller rental. If anything, it'll be a godsend at the end of the day when you're sick of lugging around those day packs!

39.

Map Savvy

Many people shy away from maps for fear of not being able to decipher or understand them. But maps remain one of the most important parts of a vacation—whether that vacation takes you on a road trip, out for a day of sightseeing, or to a theme park or zoo. When you have a map in your possession, you have better control of your vacation and the key to a less-stressful experience.

In most cities and countries, urban life was not planned in an ordinary fashion. A good map, if studied ahead of time, can save valuable sightseeing, travel, and vacation time. Careful review of a map, perhaps the night before a visit or road trip, can take the fear out of the map itself and help travelers sharpen their sense of direction.

If your spouse or travel partner has an instinctively poor sense of direction, it falls on you to become the map-savvy one on the vacation. Don't take that position lightly. Memorize the layout of your map well ahead of time, and know your proposed route for the day like the back of your hand. It beats getting lost and having to ask for directions, especially if you're already struggling to speak the language!

40.

Day Trippers

Travel doesn't necessarily imply an overnight visit. For many, a fabulous day trip every now and then constitutes a great mini-vacation! Day trips can be as refreshing to the soul as a weekend away. A long day spent touring city museums, air-shuttling it to a neighboring city, or hosting a family field day on the shore can be enough of an escape for the overworked to seem as if they've been away for days. Also, day trips are almost always less expensive.

It's simple to prepare for a fantastic day trip—your first step should be to secure a wide-open date. Even if you only plan on going a few miles from home for the day, devote every waking hour to getting to and from your destination and enjoying your time spent there as much as possible.

Call ahead and investigate transportation schedules, attraction hours, and admission prices. If you plan on taking public transportation, ease your mind regarding your return by pre-selecting the train or bus on which you hope to return.

Obviously, if your day out and about includes museum or zoo visits, you won't need to prepare an extensive day pack—just some light snacks and bottled water for everyone, maps, some antibacterial wipes, and a cell phone. If you're traveling with young children, bring along a stroller, too. But if you intend to entertain yourselves for the full day—say at a beach or park—a proper cooler-bag and supply pack is necessary.

Barbecuing is always a good bet for a large group that will be eating outdoors together. Many meals can be prepared ahead of time and grilled later—even chicken nuggets and pizza can be reheated on a barbecue grill. Check to see if you'll be using an electric or gas grill where you'll be eating, and see if you'll need charcoal and lighter fluid. Remember to pack along extra foil wrap, paper plates, eating utensils, napkins, paper towels, cups, and matches. Pack all items that could possibly leak in resealable plastic containers.

By the time that you've packed the car for your day trip, it may feel as if you're packing for a weeklong vacation. But better to arrive prepared for anything than to have to leave all the fun and go in search of something you know that you could have taken along!

41.

Organize
Your Day Bag

There's nothing in the world like vacationing with an efficient day pack, being prepared for whatever life on the run brings you. Never confuse your day pack with your suitcase or money belt. Your suitcase should stay in your hotel room where it belongs for the duration of your trip, and your money belt should stay on your person at all times, with your passport, credit cards and important papers inside. You should never keep any of those things in your day pack.

Your day pack should be lightweight when empty and comfortable to carry, with thick zipper closures, and preferably a flap covering the zipper to deter would-be pickpockets. If you're traveling without children, your bag for the day should contain, in addition to maps and antibacterial wipes, travel guides and brochures; your glasses case; two zipper bags; a camera with an extra roll of film; a pen and small memo pad or journal; a net shopping bag; moisturizer or sunblock; a pocketknife (though not if you're going on an airplane); lip balm; a hat for sun protection; bottled water; snacks; disposable rain ponchos; insect repellent; and toilet paper. It sounds like more than it really is!

If you have children, however, you'll need to add some, if not all, of these items (a diaper bag that can be worn on the back makes an excellent day pack for traveling with kids): diapers and cleaning wipes; two plastic bags; a cloth diaper for a changing pad; extra snacks and water; a small toy to keep them entertained; antibacterial ointment and colorful adhesive bandages; a pacifier (optional); a favorite doll or blanket; kid-sized disposable rain ponchos; and baby sunblock.

When shopping for these items, consider the fact that you're going to be carrying them around all day, every day. Choose products that are the lightest in weight or that come in the smallest packs or bottles.

Most important, remember that the key word to buying travel items is "disposable." When you're finished with it, toss it and make your day pack lighter as the day goes on!

42.

Getting What
You Paid For

For travel throughout the world (with the exception of Asia), your hotel stay will probably eat up the largest portion of your vacation budget! Some travel experts advise that one way to beat the high-priced hotel rates abroad is to book only your first night's reservation ahead of time. Once you arrive, look for a smaller, less expensive accommodation. The small neighborhood hotels not only have lower rates, but can have a lot more to offer by way of charm and personal service.

Your hotel room can make or break your vacation. Always ask to see the room before you take it. In fact, in many countries, this is a standard practice. Make sure that it's clean, well-equipped, and located in a satisfactory, safe part of the hotel. Check to make sure that the heat or air conditioning works, which windows and drapes open and close, that there is a fire alarm or sprinkler system, and that there are locks on the door. If you aren't happy with the room, ask for another one—or ask for a price reduction if it does not meet your standards.

One prominent travel writer urges hotel-bound consumers to ask the hotel clerk five questions before heading up to the room: If there is hotel construction taking place and how close the room is to it; how far the room is from the hotel ballroom (to avoid being awakened in the wee hours of the night by cleanup staff); how close the room is to the elevators (for safety and noise); if the hotel heating is a two-pipe or four-pipe system (you want four-pipe); and which floors have booster pumps. This last question is in response to a recent survey of travelers who revealed that a hotel's water pressure is the single most important thing to them during a hotel stay. The clerk should be able to place a call to engineering to determine which floors have booster pumps. You want a room on one of those floors.

Another important tip from this travel writer is that once you've entered your room, ask the hotel staff to remove the bedspreads. Hotels do not wash the bedspreads in between guests. Finally, when your room is satisfactory upon inspection, you can begin to settle in.

Be sure to investigate the various hotel charges at this time, too —or you'll be in for a big surprise upon receiving your bill at checkout. Telephone charges can be astronomical. Be aware of room service charges, hotel safe charges, minibar charges, cable television and in-room movie charges, and fax and overnight delivery charges. You may want to find out about waiving delivery charges with the hotel clerk ahead of time if you know that you're going to be receiving packages or faxes.

Your total satisfaction with your hotel stay is an essential part of your vacation. Think of how much money it is costing you to stay there! Remember that everything is negotiable (especially your room rate), and everything is possible — as long as you speak up and ask for it!

43.

Holiday Travel Without the Horror

The holidays are a wonderful time to see family and friends, especially when you haven't seen each other for a while. For many, this means a road trip, a rail excursion, or a plane ride. Unfortunately, holiday time is the worst time to be on the road, on the rails, or in the air, for the simple reason that everyone is traveling and everyone is anxious to get to their destination. Traffic, airport congestion, weather hazards, and tired travelers all make for one dangerous travel situation.

Safety should be included in all your travel plans during the holidays, no matter how you choose to travel. If your holiday travel is by car, obtain and correctly install any necessary child-safety seats. (By law, children under forty pounds need to ride in a child car seat, but the actual rules and regulations for that differ from place to place.) If your child is too big for a child seat, he or she still needs to be fastened securely in a seat other than the front passenger seat. Other car safety hazards — especially at holiday time — include loose luggage or gift boxes packed on the back window shelf of the car. These items can severely injure a child riding just below them should the vehicle come to an abrupt stop. They can also block your rear view. Don't forget that when driving for an extended length of time, it's very important to take a rest every two hours to let your kids unwind and allow yourself an opportunity to stretch.

When you're planning to travel by air for the holidays, be sure to tell the travel agent that you're traveling with children. Many airlines will try to keep the seats next to you empty or give you a bulkhead seat. Ask for a seat in the middle of the plane — these are always the last to be sold. If they aren't sold (though chances are that during holiday times, they probably will be sold out), you'll have a seat for your child. Also, check with the airline regarding policies on the use of a child- or infant-safety seat. Different airlines have different policies, and you may need to bring one along.

Basically, the key to successful holiday travel by any means is to keep children constantly occupied, stimulated, and fed! Portable electronic games, activity and puzzle books, and travel-sized board games are great for keeping children entertained on long trips. In fact, during holiday times, bring along double the amount of stuff for your kids, since there are sure to be long airport delays and traffic jams.

Should the whining and complaining reach an all-time high, just take a deep breath and count to ten. Then smile, remind yourself about the true meaning of the holidays, and think about the joyous quality time that you'll soon be spending together.

44.

Combating Jet Lag

You know how the first days in a new time zone can be: You're sleepy all day, but when it's time to sleep, you toss and turn or sleep fitfully. You spend most of the first few days sightseeing in a foggy state of mind—even avoiding occasions to go on a tour or take a walk, despite the fact that you're visiting for the purpose of touring.

Some researchers say that for every time zone you cross, it takes one full day for your body to adjust. Scientists call jet lag a disruption of the circadian rhythm—the daily individual cycle of sleep and wakefulness.

Unfortunately, travelers have traditionally battled this problem with naps, sleeping pills, or self-medication with caffeine and alcohol. There are healthier ways that can be just as effective.

Try resetting your watch to the destination's time as soon as you get on the airplane. If it's daytime in your new destination, try to stay awake. Walk around the cabin to keep yourself alert. When it's nighttime in your destination point, try to sleep. Try to stay awake until at least eleven at night, destination time—that will give you ample time to sleep and get your new cycle into gear. Use a sleeping mask and earplugs to help block out noise and light on the plane.

Eat before you get on the plane. This way, neither your growling stomach nor dinner service will distract you from sleep. Just be sure to tell the attendant ahead of time that you don't need to be awakened for a meal. Buckling your seat belt over your blanket is a good idea, too, so that the flight attendant will not have to wake you in the event of turbulence.

If you're not sleepy, there are ways to get sleepy. Reading for a little while can often help you feel tired, and so can working on a crossword puzzle. Don't drink alcohol—even if you think that it will make you sleepy or ease your anxiety over flying. Drinking alcohol at a high altitude—while you're anxious and tense—may only make you sick to your stomach.

If it's daylight when you arrive at your hotel but nighttime at home, you may be tempted to "take a little nap." Instead, try going for a walk outside. The exercise may revive you, and daylight should help convince your body to stop producing sleep-inducing hormones.

45.

How to Do...

Nothing!

For many, one of the most difficult parts of a vacation is simply the act of relaxing! After all of the researching, planning, organizing, phone calls, packing, arrangements, and travel anxiety, by the time we're actually lounging in that lounge chair, many of us are frustrated to find that our minds are still racing, our hearts are still thumping...and amazingly, we're beginning to stress over the trip home.

Those of us vacationing for the sole purpose of relaxation need to learn the steps involved in doing just that. Relaxing doesn't just mean settling in a lounge chair and hoping for the best. Like your concentrated planning for the vacation itself, relaxing, too, must be organized.

Anticipate your need to decompress on day one of your vacation. Don't plan any exerting activity for the first day. Instead, arrange for a little pampering—sleep late, get a massage, partake in a satisfying continental breakfast, go for an early morning swim or take a walk along the beach. Indulge only in activities that you completely enjoy or have participated in before, to minimize the stress often associated with trying new things.

Make time for yourself! Even if you've got four active kids in tow, arrange with your spouse for an hour or two of alone time where you can really get your tired body to relax. Just remember to give your spouse the same consideration, and promise to supervise the kids for a while so he or she can take some time alone, as well.

Avoid caffeine at the start of your first vacation day. Find a warm, comfortable, secluded spot to settle in, and try yoga, stretching exercises, or meditation. Bury yourself in a good book, and remind yourself to stop and take deep, relaxing breaths every so often. Don't think about the activities that you're missing, the sites you're not seeing, or the plans you're not making for the next day. There will be time for that much later, after you've relaxed enough to begin to enjoy yourself.

46.

There's No Business
Like a Business Trip!

The travel industry is heavily interested and invested in the travel needs of the business traveler. Business travelers log in long miles, numerous hotel stays, and a steady stream of business meals day in and out. They often pay too much for their seats on the plane and the highest hotel rates imaginable, and their expense account accommodates the most expensive meals. It makes sense that the travel industry caters to their needs.

But because the industry assumes that every business traveler operates with a large budget, it's harder for small business travelers without big expense accounts to find bargain rates or attractive discounts. Uncovering a good rate for your business travel plans requires some flexibility—like agreeing to stay over on a Saturday night, for example—and some clever research techniques.

As with recreational travelers, if you want a discount, you'll have to ask for one! There is almost always a corporate discount available—one that most hotels and airlines won't mention. Sometimes, if you're open to combining your business trip with some leisure travel, extending your trip to include the weekend and bringing a friend along can actually work out costing less than your original fare! As amazing as it seems, your willingness to stay over on a Saturday night can cut your air fare almost seventy percent! Because of this, a number of corporations are encouraging their workers to include the weekend in their travel plans, and bring their spouse or significant other along for a mini-vacation.

The result? Happy employees, happy spouses, and hefty company profits, not to mention happy hotel owners!

47.

More Unconventional Vacations

Did you ever think that you could make a difference in the world just by going on vacation? Though not entirely free, "volunteer vacations" reward your labors with significantly lower prices. While many volunteer vacations require that you pay your own transportation, often the lodging and meal costs are picked up by the organization for which you're volunteering.

For most of these trips, you live and work with other volunteers —a plus for those looking to meet new and interesting people. The work required is often somewhere between four and eight hours a day, and you may have to commit to three or four weeks of work, but by spending your days performing socially conscious acts, you'll enjoy a deep inner satisfaction, in addition to the savings.

Many such volunteer programs are offered to students, but not exclusively—all ages are usually accepted. There are organizations who send volunteers to some seventy countries around the world to aid with construction, social work, and environmental projects, such as restoring streams, planting trees, or working in national parks. Other organizations take volunteers on a one- to three-week trip to one of nineteen nations to participate in such worthy tasks as caring for children in orphanages, teaching English, improving water systems, and working at cultural festivals. For all of these programs, meals, lodging, and in-country transportation is completely covered.

Similarly, "impact vacations" offer vacationers trips with a conscience. Daily excursions usually involve sightseeing and taking in the scenery, but also add a "day of impact" where participants visit a social service or environmental organization. Projects range from assisting the terminally ill to feeding the homeless to cultural preservation.

Rates for impact vacations include lodging, meals, gear, and entry fees, but can often run very high. If it's altruistic joy and fulfillment that you seek on your next vacation, rebuilding houses or assisting in medical clinics will bring you the sense of "giving back" that you crave.

48.

First Class Act

Believe it or not, the space in airplane coach cabins during recent years has become even more cramped. While many airlines are spending money making first class and business class more comfortable for their higher paying customers, the lower priced seats are losing out on precious space. Newer planes even have more seats crammed into coach, resulting in far less reclining space or legroom.

But don't rush to reserve seats in those forward cabins just yet! Do a little investigating before shelling out the big bucks for a first class ticket. In some airlines, there isn't really much difference between coach and first class. They may offer only slightly more leg room and a little extra added storage space in the overhead bin in first class, though they'll still charge double or triple for a ticket. The food is only slightly better in first class, too. So be cautious before parting with your money. Ask the ticket agent to tell you the distance between seats in first class, and the distance between seats in coach. (On some airlines this difference is only an inch or so.) You may also want to ask how far the first-class seats recline. On some airlines, first class seats only recline a bit more than seats in coach. On other airlines, you may find your seat reclines completely. But you'll never know unless you ask. And if your travel plans include a long haul up in the air—your comfort should be your top priority.

One solution is to join a frequent flier club that awards you mileage points every time that you fly. It also offers a comfortable lounge at most airports where you can have complimentary coffee and a more relaxing atmosphere to wait for your flight. Use your mileage points to upgrade your class status. Many of the mileage points that people accumulate remain unused, resulting in lots of extra revenue for the airlines and little benefit for the consumer. If you have extra points, use them to upgrade to business class. The extra inches that your seat will recline—resulting in a more relaxed you upon arrival—is reason enough!

49.

Taking Kitty Along

If you're headed on vacation and just can't bear to leave your cat or dog behind, you're not alone. It's estimated that each year, millions of pet owners bring their furry friends with them on vacation. But before you put your pet in the car or on the plane, be aware of the risks involved and how they relate to your desired mode of travel.

Transporting pets by car is common practice these days, but because many pet owners neglect to properly restrain their animals, there are numerous reports of animals causing car accidents by distracting their owners while driving. That said, it is still possible for your pet to join you on the family vacation — if you regard the law and transport your pet in a way that's both safe and comfortable for everyone.

The most approved method of transport (suggested by veterinarians) is a pet kennel fastened by a seat belt to keep it from shifting. Others prefer a specifically designed pet seat belt, which can be effective, but can also be darn near impossible to get onto an active puppy or kitten.

Transporting your pet safely by air is a more involved process. While most animals travel in cargo bins below the cabin, small pets are usually permitted to ride with their owners in the cabin. This will be an extra cost, and different airlines have limits on how many pets they allow to travel on one flight in the cabin. Pets, large or small, are prohibited in the cabin on international flights. Many pet owners who are traveling internationally ship their pets in the forward, climate-controlled cargo bins. This costs extra, too.

It's also worth mentioning that there are dangers involved with transporting pets by plane. There is always the chance that your pet will be loaded into the wrong cargo bin—something that can become deadly when temperatures drop in some parts of the lower airplane. Higher temperatures and summer travel also pose a threat to animals riding in cargo. The time that animals sometimes spend in the cargo hold before takeoff or after landing can lead to serious injuries or death, particularly if flights are delayed. Because of this, some airlines refuse to accept live animals if temperatures on a trip rise above eighty-five degrees. If you simply must ship your pet and you cannot find an airline to accommodate you, ask your veterinarian for a local commercial shipper and animal breeder who can safely transport your pet.

Once you're away, vacationing with a pet has certain restrictions, depending on where you are traveling. You'll need to find hotels, museums, parks, and restaurants that are pet-friendly. Travel guides offer addresses and phone numbers of accommodations that accept pets—make hotel reservations at two different places before leaving on your vacation, should one not meet your approval upon arrival. There are some travel guides that cater exclusively to traveling with pets. With the proper planning, you can minimize your stress while on your next "family" vacation.

50.

Are Traveler's Checks
a Thing of the Past?

With the majority of credit cards now accepted at more locations around the world, and with many of these same countries also recognizing our ATM system, it may seem that the need for purchasing traveler's checks for travel abroad has diminished. But having your money in traveler's checks still remains the safest way to bring money abroad. Plus traveler's checks often receive a better exchange rate than cash!

In some countries, however, traveler's checks are more expensive to cash. Research exchange rates before you leave home, and learn about the recognized forms of currency in the countries that you plan on visiting. It may not make sense for you to convert all of your money into traveler's checks. Plus if the dollar is sinking as you're making your preparations, you may wish to take a gamble and purchase your traveler's checks in the currency of your destination to "fix" your exchange rate. Keep in mind, however, that the dollar may suddenly rise again.

The U.S. State Department recommends bringing most of your money abroad in traveler's checks—and remembering to record the serial numbers, denominations, and dates, and the location of the issuing bank or agency—just in case they get lost or stolen. It's also a good idea to vary your denominations. You'll want smaller denominations so that you won't lose out on a bad exchange rate, and large denominations so that you're not constantly cashing checks, standing on line at a bank or American Express office. Finally, remember that you'll almost always need your passport in order to cash your traveler's checks—whether you cash them at a bank, an American Express office, or a museum, shop, or restaurant.

51.

Memorizing the
Exchange Rate

As a traveler, knowing the exchange rates of certain destinations can give you an insight as to which countries are most favorable with respect to the American dollar. In some cases, knowing the exchange rate can even be the deciding factor as to where you'll be vacationing! Exchange rates are also important in helping you determine the value of items that you wish to purchase while abroad.

Once you determine where to go, and before you leave for your trip, do two things: First, visit a web site that offers an instant currency converter—you can instantaneously view updated exchange rates for 165 countries with just a click. Second, order the equivalent of fifty to one hundred dollars in the currency of your destination through your bank. You won't get a great exchange rate, but it will save you the hassle of arriving in a foreign country and having to immediately cope with finding the nearest bank.

Once you're settled in at your hotel, do a little detective work to find the best rate of exchange. ATMs, local banks, or American Express and Thomas Cook offices usually give decent exchange rates. In some countries, shopkeepers or locals will give you an excellent exchange rate—but that black-market exchange is often illegal. The bottom line is to avoid exchanging dollars at your hotel—hotels almost always offer the worst exchange rates there are.

It's important for travelers abroad to familiarize themselves with the country's currency. Take a close look at the foreign coins and bills, and figure out how to tell them apart. You'll want to be familiar enough with them so that you can quickly calculate the value of souvenirs or determine if the taxi driver is taking you for a ride. Remember also that loose change does not always convert back to U.S. currency, so do your best to use up all of your coins before breaking another bill.

Further minimize your stress levels by preparing for the trip home and saving all of the receipts from the money that you change. Many countries require you to show your receipts if you want to convert your money back to dollars. They do this to ensure that you aren't making money by exchanging through the black market.

52.

Are You
Euro-Ready?

In early 2002, the euro became legal tender for twelve member nations of the European Monetary Union. If you are traveling to Europe anytime soon, you may wonder what this change means for you.

Great Britain, Denmark, Sweden, and Russia have *not* converted their currencies to the euro. The twelve participating countries are Austria, Belgium, Finland, France, Germany, Greece, Ireland, Italy, Luxembourg, the Netherlands, Portugal, and Spain. European countries not listed will continue to use their own currencies.

After June 30, 2002, you can only exchange leftover currency for euros at national central banks—you will not be able to use it for transactions. The introduction of the euro will not affect your ability to use your credit card for purchases and cash withdrawals. Your credit card bill will reflect your transactions according to the exchange rate at the time that they were made.

Your ATM card will still be accepted in the places that it was accepted before, but in countries that have switched over to the euro, your withdrawal will be in euros. Like your credit card bill, your bank statement will reflect your withdrawal according to the exchange rate at the time of your withdrawal.

Despite the convenience of one currency, you should still make it a point to know the exchange rate in each country you visit. You should also expect some fluctuation in the value of the euro from country to country, depending on where you are.

Consider bringing along a pocket calculator to speed this process along—especially if you're planning on doing some shopping. Learn how the exchange system works, too—deciphering the buy and sell charts posted in banks for your convenience can in actuality be an all-day activity. Know the operating hours of the banks that you plan on using. Banks in other countries tend to have fewer—and stranger—hours than they do in the United States. Many banks close for an hour or two at noon, and in some countries, banks close for a week or more during "banking holidays."

A word of advice to save you a lot of stress at the ATM machine in Europe—make sure before leaving home that your Personal Identification Number (PIN) for cash withdrawals on your ATM or credit card is just four digits. European ATMs require a four-digit PIN number code. If your PIN is more than four digits, change it before your trip!

53.

Où Est la Restroom?

It's common knowledge that the one thing about Americans that foreigners deeply resent is a tourist who assumes that everyone speaks English. It stands to reason that you will get around a lot better in a foreign country if you try to speak the native language—at least a little of it. People everywhere will greatly appreciate the effort.

Of course, there's no way you can possibly learn to speak the language of every country that you'll ever visit, but you can learn enough to get by, to order dinner, and to make friends with the natives. If you start to learn at home, you'll pick up even more while you're away. Learning a foreign language is easiest when you're immersed in it and surrounded by people who are speaking it.

There are many things that you can do at home in order to help you learn to speak a new language. You can head over to your local library and take out instructional language cassettes and books. Play the tapes while you drive around to familiarize yourself with the language's pronunciations and rhythms.

Online dictionaries are very helpful, too. Prepare yourself a list of one hundred words or terms that you hope to learn, and then work on memorizing five to ten a day.

Handheld electronic translators work just fine, too—most are preprogrammed with all of the familiar phrases and questions that you'll need to ask while away. Possible answers can be translated, too.

If there's enough time before your vacation, and you plan on being in one country for a while, consider attending a language course or hiring a tutor. A tutor can help you familiarize yourself with accents and pronunciation while you study grammar and tenses on your own. Instructional language teachers can also add a little cultural flavor to lessons to prepare you for making the most of your trip.

When you finally arrive in the foreign country that you've been preparing so diligently to visit, don't be embarrassed to speak! You're going to make mistakes, but you'll be surprised to see how quickly it comes when you have some eager subjects on whom to test your new speaking skills!

54.

Off the Beaten Path

The phrase "off the beaten path" came about in a popular travel guide years ago, when it became apparent that many readers were heeding the editor's advice and staying at the same suggested hotels, visiting the same attractions, and eating at the same restaurants that they read about. "Off the beaten path" became a reference term for attractions, hotels, restaurants, and shops that aren't commonly visited by tourists.

If you're interested in visiting little-known, less-traveled sites the next time that you're vacationing, make your own beaten path, and then step off it to explore! Walk into a shop or restaurant and converse with the staff. Ask them for suggestions as to places that they recommend you should go. Find out where the natives shop, eat, and play and you're likely to be surprised. The prices at local places will probably be less expensive than the more popular tourist traps.

Taxi drivers are some of the best sources of information! Taxi drivers know more about the area they work in than anyone else.

Take safety precautions when you're headed off the beaten path. Just because a place is recommended doesn't mean that it is going to be in a safe area. Make arrangements with a driver if you're headed to a new place, and ask to be taken right to the door. The driver should stay until you're sure that you can get inside, and in some circumstances, pick you up at a predetermined time to take you back to your hotel. It's a fabulous experience to explore new things on your own, but always proceed along the beaten path while exercising caution.

55.

Don't Stress over
a Change of Plans

The inevitable change of plans—it's happened to all of us. Letting it get to you, however, is the worst thing that you can do, and it will almost always spoil your vacation fun.

For many, creating a vacation itinerary and sticking to it is an absolute necessity. Tourists like these are truly wonderful to travel with—they work hard at orchestrating the most elaborate travel plans—but they are certainly not the most flexible people.

Travelers who realize this about themselves can help themselves by creating backup plans should problems arise. Frustration associated with glitches in your itinerary can lead to disappointment and stress. There are other steps besides backup plans that you can take to alleviate any bad feelings you may experience, as well. First, be sure to schedule downtime into your itinerary. Schedule it in the late afternoon—should a mishap occur in the morning, your daily schedule can be moved ahead and nothing will be missed. Without problems, your downtime can be used to rest, spend more time at the previous activity, or just shop for souvenirs.

Next, teach yourself some helpful deep-breathing exercises to relax and regain control. Use the exercise time to remind yourself that people are not robots and can't always be expected to stick to a schedule. If you're traveling with children, they may need to catch up on sleep one morning or just run around a local park.

Resist the urge to prepare your daily itinerary alone. Ask your group for input. Always have an alternative method of transportation or a second time of departure to your destination. This way, if there's a bus strike or a track problem, you'll still have transportation options.

Every time we vacation with expectations, there's a good chance that some plan will go awry. The key to survival is to make the best of every situation—and remain in control of yourself. Experiencing anxiety and stress on your vacation is a lot more detrimental than experiencing a little registration mix-up at your hotel.

56.

Your Extended Stay

There's no greater feeling than the excitement associated with leaving for vacation. But often, you may be let down if your cherished plans do not live up to your expectations. Of course, one thing you can do to avoid this is lower your expectations. But for the amount of money that you may be spending, it stands to reason that you should indeed have high expectations that you'll have an amazing time.

Perhaps a better idea would be to keep your expectations realistic. Get rid of all of your preconceived notions about what to expect on vacation, and just go with the flow! So the cabin is a lot smaller than the brochure pictured it to be—make the most of it anyway. Chances are that you won't be spending too much time in the cabin anyway. Perhaps the food isn't all that it's been cracked up to be. So what? Food is just food—it shouldn't make or break your trip.

More important even than adapting that carefree vacation outlook is to make sure that you put aside a little time each day to really revel in your surroundings. Take a good look at where you are and who you're with. Appreciate the moments together, free from life's commitments—and the chance to really enjoy each other's company. Work, school, and daily activities get in the way of spending quality time with our family and friends. Vacations—no matter where you spend them—offer the perfect opportunity to fill your days with exciting adventures and stimulating activities and to share them with the people that you love most in the world.

57.

"Are We There Yet?"

G ot kids? Then chances are you've heard those words before: "Are we there yet?" Even parents with a high threshold for patience cringe when they hear those words. It's not the words themselves that are so bothersome. It's the frequency with which they're spoken!

There are ways, however, to minimize the frequency of this question during your vacation road or plane trips. All it takes is some planning ahead.

The next time that you're about to go on a vacation or a trip where a longer-than-usual car ride is required, why not try outlining your travel route in a way that your children can follow? Try providing each of your children with their own map that has your travel route from point to point highlighted. Give them each a marker to mark off exits or sights along the way so that they can keep track of the trip themselves. This way, they'll be able to "see" exactly where they are and they'll know whether they're there yet or not!

Don't rely solely on this. Following your car trip route can be fun for short periods of time every so often, but it's not something that can keep children occupied for longer periods of time. Ensure that they take along enough fun activities to hold their attention. A few days before you leave, bring your children to a bookstore or department store that sells travel games. Help them pick out activity books and small, lightweight travel games that are age-appropriate. You don't have to spend a fortune, but think about it this way: How much is it worth to you to avoid the dreaded question, "Are we there yet?"

58.

The Perfect *Un*packing

You've made it! The long trip is over, you've inspected your accommodations and checked in, and now you're ready to unpack. What you do in the next half hour can, in fact, determine the stress factor for the rest of your trip!

Travelers fall into two categories: compulsive organizers and those who let things fall where they may. For the best possible vacation scenario, you should strive to place yourself somewhere in the middle.

Compulsive organizers completely unpack within the first few minutes of tipping the baggage person. They have drawers designated for everybody and everything, closet space claimed and immediately utilized, sink space allotted and arranged—they've even chosen their side of the bed, and claimed the extra blanket before their travel companions manage to unpack a thing.

The other sort of traveler lives out of his or her suitcase for a day or so before unpacking. These people are almost always in wrinkled clothes and their toothbrushes lie flat on the bathroom counter instead of upright in a hotel-provided glass. What *they're* most interested in upon check-in is not ample drawer space or close proximity to the ice maker, but checking out the room service menu and finding where the chambermaid has hidden the remote.

It is a good idea to unpack upon arrival—especially if your clothes have been sitting in your suitcase for hours. Pay attention to your nicest clothing first—you may even need to iron one or two items before hanging them up. Better to do it now than five minutes before you're hoping to wear them.

If you're traveling with other adults, be sure to unpack your own things and put them away in a spot that's convenient for you. If you're traveling with children, unpack their belongings first and be careful to make their things the most available. Children on vacation change clothes more than a few times a day, and it can be cumbersome to reach for bottom drawers all the time.

Claim your bathroom space early on—though don't allow it to be a source of arguments. Be fair and compromising—remember that you're going to be sharing close quarters for an extended period of time. Set your toiletries in an easily accessible area, keeping them out of reach of children. Many parents forget that hotel rooms are not childproof.

Most important, respect the privacy of others. It can be a great source of stress for many people to have their personal belongings so accessible to others. Even more stressful than having a noisy roommate is sharing living space with an inconsiderate person.

59.

Lost Luggage Anxiety

It's estimated that 2 million bags circulate through airport carousels on any given day. During high-peak travel times like holidays, that number nearly doubles! It's hard to believe that the number of suitcases lost, misdirected, or damaged by the airlines is actually pretty low.

But if you're a frequent traveler, sooner or later the time may come when you'll be forced to deal with the hassle of lost luggage. Though the majority of lost bags are returned to their owners within twenty-four hours, it makes sense for travelers to take necessary precautions to minimize the chances of their bags becoming lost, routed to the wrong airport, or damaged in transit. The next time that you pack for a trip, anticipate the worst-case scenario. Never pack cash, valuables, important documents, or breakables in your luggage!

Every single piece of luggage you travel with should be clearly marked with an ID tag. While it helps to travel with a set of matching luggage for easy identification, if you happen to have a bunch of different suitcases, consider tying the same color ribbon to each bag so that you'll be able to pick them out of the pile of bags making their way around the conveyor belt.

When you make your airline reservations, avoid changing airlines if you can, especially if you are making a connection. The more complicated your itinerary is, the more likely it is that your bags will get lost! If you simply must travel on different airlines, consider shipping your bags ahead of time! There are companies that specialize in door-to-door transportation of your luggage.

But what should you do if despite your best efforts, your luggage becomes lost anyway? Try to remain calm. Most luggage is delayed, not permanently lost. File a missing luggage form immediately— even if you're told that your bags will arrive on the next flight. Don't leave the airport without a copy of the report, and the airline's claims department phone number.

If you need an item in your bag right away, many airlines will reimburse you if you purchase that item. Some may even give you a cash advance to purchase it. Find out what your airline's reimbursement policy is. Most airlines allow leisure travelers to buy a new wardrobe and then reimburse them later. For business travelers with lost luggage, there are airlines that advance them cash to replace the needed items immediately. Airlines usually offer a daily stipend of twenty-five to fifty dollars for items such as toiletries, and some airlines have ready-made kits to give out for this purpose.

There's nothing worse than watching an empty conveyor belt go around, hoping that your luggage will just suddenly appear. Whether you're traveling for business or pleasure, take the proper steps every time that you go to prevent this scenario from happening to you!

60.

The Sightseeing
Checklist

An essential part of vacationing is finding and reviewing the perfect vacation travel guide. A bible of sorts, the vacation travel guide is usually your most important travel companion—encompassing all of the research, facts, and anecdotes sweated over in preparation for a trip.

For many, reading a travel guide creates a low-stress way to travel. For others, planning every second of their vacation and reading about every sight beforehand ruins their experience. They'd rather experience the sights on their own and form their own opinions.

Whichever is your travel MO, it stands to reason that developing a sightseeing checklist is a must. If you don't determine beforehand what you would like to see and where you wish to go, you could very well be overwhelmed once you're there, with too many options to choose from.

When so many great choices are presented, it becomes the task of the vacationer to determine what is and what isn't worth visiting. If you're a travel guide devotee, get yourself a highlighter pen and use your traveling time (on the plane, in the car, on the train, whatever) to narrow down the long list of sights that you hope to visit. Consider the travel time needed to see them all, and then plan your destinations accordingly. Even if you're not a fan of travel guides, it helps to leaf through one before your trip and make a list of all of the sights that you hope to see, in order from most important to least.

Keep in mind that just because a certain sight was a must-see for some does not mean that it's a must-see for you. Resist the urge to visit a museum or park that you have little interest in, just because you've read or heard that it's the trendy place to go. Instead, include only your absolute must-sees on your agenda. This is your vacation experience. Even if you follow your travel guide religiously, make the trip your experience. The result will be even more satisfying than having seen it all!

61.

"The Louvre, Again?"

If you're considering traveling to Europe with your children, there are some minor alterations to make to your trip that will ensure a successful vacation for all. This is not to suggest that you have to forgo fine art and culture just yet. Kid-friendly Europe has all that—and then some. You just have to know where to find it!

In London, for example, visit the historical sights your children may have read about in works of fiction. Kids will also love a jaunt through an English hedge maze or down into a real coal mine. Most major European cities have magazines devoted to sightseeing with children. Look for them at an international newsstand when you're planning your trip.

You won't hear a whine or complaint from your kids if you take them through the Chunnel either. This three-hour train ride under the English Channel ends up in Paris, where your kids will love exploring prehistoric caves, locating Europe's largest sand dune, and visiting those other Parisian favorites, the Eiffel Tower and Notre Dame.

Can an eight-year-old have fun in Germany? Will your teen be bored in Milan? No way! You just have to know where to bring them. For instance, what kid (or adult) wouldn't love watching a BMW assembly line, or visiting a chocolate factory (both in Germany)? There are authentic doll museums in Switzerland, wooden shoes, windmills, and dikes in Denmark, and in southern Europe children of all ages will have great fun exploring Pinocchio's birthplace or Mount Olympus, and taking an exciting rooftop walk atop a historic cathedral.

So it's not where you go, it's where exactly you go! Save the stuffy flower garden tours and the escargot-dining experiences for another time. Instead, do a little extra legwork and research beforehand to treat your kids to a European adventure that they'll never forget!

62.

Dining Out with Kids

Parents on vacation face the bewildering task of eating almost every meal in restaurants with their children and getting them to behave. To ensure that the experiences are relaxing and rewarding, rather than exhausting and aggravating, follow a few simple rules.

Eat in whenever possible. Hopefully, you'll have enough foresight to select a hotel with a kitchen suite, or a mini-fridge and microwave. If you do, bring along some easily microwavable meals, and visit a convenience store near your hotel for the essentials: eggs, milk, butter, bread, peanut butter, and juice. There are a lot of quick meals that you can make in your hotel room, including instant macaroni and cheese and soup. For every meal that you eat in, there's one less chance for aggravation at a restaurant. It will be less stressful for your children, as well. You can always feed the kids a quick meal in your room, and then order adult food from room service. Breakfasts, lunches, and dinners can all be quick and easy in-room meals if you dread the thought of going out.

If you simply must go out to a restaurant, ask your hotel concierge to recommend a kid-friendly place. Many travel guide books, too, offer a section on restaurants that welcome children.

Don't wait until your kids are famished to dine, and don't wait until your own stomach is growling. Hunger can make anyone irritable, and starting off a meal in that state can only lead to disaster. For very young children, order their meals soon after being seated, even if you aren't ready to order for yourselves. Children get impatient and fidgety while waiting, and this way, their wait won't be so long.

Bring some crayons and a coloring book or blank paper to occupy your kids while they wait. Older children can be entertained with paper and pens to play games like hangman, tic-tac-toe, and dots.

If you find yourselves in a restaurant without a children's menu, take a look at the appetizers offered. The portions are smaller, and they usually have more appealing food for children. Order one or two for your kids to divide and share.

Use dinnertime to talk about your day—all of the places that you visited, all of the things that you did. You can even vote on which activity or sight was their favorite. Talk about where they would like to go tomorrow, and get some planning out of the way. Ask your kids if there are any places that they would like to visit again before heading home.

Dessert is always a popular part of the meal for kids. Let them know ahead of time that good behavior in the restaurant will be rewarded with a fun dessert.

Most important, relax with your children and unwind from the day. Chances are that you've walked more than usual and extended yourselves in order to fit in a full day. Use the mealtime to enjoy each other's company and refuel for what lies ahead.

63.
Bed, Breakfast,
and Bliss

There's a certain image that comes to mind when thinking about a bed and breakfast vacation: romantic, Victorian hideaways, porches, fireplaces, freshly prepared meals, and crisp comforters on every king-sized bed.

Bed and breakfast accommodations offer vacationers a unique and personalized travel experience with the perfect touch of local flavor. Most of these small, charming, privately owned lodgings are an affordable choice for either pleasure or business travel. Not too many, however, cater to families with young children. In fact, you can easily find a great B & B that will accept your Labrador retriever ahead of your five-year-old.

There isn't a corner of the world where you can't find a B & B—across the United States, in Canada, Australia, New Zealand, the U.K., Mexico, Italy, France, Spain, Thailand, and more. The Internet is an excellent source for information on bed and breakfasts. The better inns can usually be found in historic, quaint little towns or areas, rather than near family-oriented places, but should you and your family wish to stay in a B & B, ask the innkeepers what their policy is regarding children. Some allow children over twelve; some don't allow any under eighteen.

For the romantic pleasures a B & B offers, grab your honey and whisk away to one of these lovers-only locations: Santa Catalina Island, California; Newport Beach, Rhode Island; Cape Cod, Massachusetts; Sedona, Arizona; Petaluma, California; Round Top, Texas; South Haven, Michigan; Middleburg, Virginia; New Hope, Pennsylvania; Cape May, New Jersey; Montauk, Long Island, New York; Grand Rapids, Ohio; Chesapeake City, Maryland; Newfound Lake, New Hampshire; and New London, Connecticut. From home, search for the perfect B & B, and you'll have the beginnings of an authentic B & B vacation!

64.

What Is Montezuma's Revenge?

In Mexico, it's called Montezuma's Revenge. In Egypt, it's Tutankhamen's Curse, and in India, it's Delhi's Belly. Silly names, but for not so silly an ailment. There's nothing funny about traveler's diarrhea (TD). The World Health Organization estimates that between twenty and fifty percent of the millions of people who travel each year become affected by it.

TD can not only ruin a vacation or business trip, it can sometimes lead to more serious complications. Usually triggered by poor sanitary conditions and acquired through the ingestion of contaminated food or water, it can be further aggravated by factors such as fatigue, jet lag, and a change in diet or climate. Symptoms of TD (which can last from three to seven days) include diarrhea, nausea, abdominal cramps, bloating, fever, and malaise. TD is most common in the developing countries of Africa, the Middle East, Asia, and Latin America. Resorts in these areas have water purification systems, but it still pays to take precautions.

There are several ways to avoid and treat the symptoms brought on by TD. Include a bottle of Pepto-Bismol (or a similar product) along on every trip you make. If you're visiting one of the countries mentioned above, it may even be a good idea to take a daily dose of Pepto while you're there as a preventative measure.

Drink only bottled water or water that has been vigorously boiled for several minutes. Allow it to cool before drinking, and remember *not* to include ice cubes, as they may not have been purified or boiled. Don't brush your teeth with tap water, either.

Check your beverages to make sure that they are topped off with a seal. Brand-name canned or bottled drinks are usually safe, but be careful to wipe the surface area of the can or bottle — it may have come in contact with contaminated water. Infants should only be given formula that has been prepared with boiled bottled water.

Be selective where you dine! Food needs to be handled with care — raw meat, shellfish, salads, and fresh fruits may be hazardous to your health.

Check with your doctor before traveling to a foreign country that has a problem with water purification. He or she can suggest the right medication for you to bring along. If you do become ill with TD while away, it's important to immediately replace the fluids and salts that your body has lost. Many countries offer oral rehydration solutions (ORS) and sell them at pharmacies and supermarkets. You can make your own solution by mixing six teaspoons of sugar and one teaspoon of salt with one liter of safe water.

Follow these tips right from the get-go should you become stricken with TD on vacation. The sooner you ward off intestinal distress, the sooner you'll be able to enjoy the rest of your vacation.

65.

A Table for Four

Many travelers plan their trips with others—for the joy of experiencing new places and cultures together, but mostly for the company another couple or family can offer. It's always wonderful to experience new places, and even better to do it with friends.

If you're traveling alone, meeting people and making new friends on the trip can be extremely exciting. For this reason, it's sometimes beneficial to travel with an organized tour group. Without the added pressure of planning and organizing, there is a lot of free time left to develop relationships with other group members. Couples can meet other couples, families with kids can meet other families with kids, and sometimes these new friendships can last a lifetime.

While making friends on vacation remains a perfectly pleasant experience, there are often obstacles that come up in a setting such as this. Differences of opinion and interest can sometimes interfere with having a pleasurable time. It's important for travelers to remember—especially when traveling in tour groups—that each family or couple in the group has spent time and money planning their vacation, and they've come with the hopes of participating in an experience that's personal to them.

Avoid dining together for every meal, or sitting together for every bus ride. You'll want to meet other people, too, and you may be perceived as unfriendly and cliquish if you stay with one other couple or family the entire time. Make sure that you spend time alone with your loved ones. Give new friends space, and they'll be sure to give you your space, too. Treat these new relationships with respect during the vacation, and you may find that you'll have travel companions for many years to come!

66.

Self-Timers Are a Must!

For many, vacation photographs are sacred. Cameras are taken along on each and every outing, and special photographs are set in special, honored places back at home. People love to pore over their vacation photos often, recalling the places visited and the great times had. For these reasons, they take care and go to great lengths to get the perfect vacation photos!

All amateur photographers can heed a few simple tips from the pros to improve the quality of their photos. But before you begin snapping away at everything in sight, take a moment to be sure that you have a good vacation camera and the right film.

A good vacation camera doesn't necessarily mean an expensive one. The perfect camera to bring on vacation is one that is compact and lightweight, and has automatic focus, panorama, zoom, and self-timing features.

Film varies according to its ISO number, which describes its speed or sensitivity to light. Film that is ISO 400 is faster and more responsive than film that is ISO 100. Simply put, if you're going to be shooting outdoors in the sun for most of your roll, a film of ISO 100 is fine. If you're shooting on a foggy day or indoors, you'll want to have ISO 400.

Try not to pose your friends and family—the same old feigned smile and unnatural pose can get boring. Instead, take candid shots, preferably of people in the shade, to avoid unattractive shadows on their faces.

Parades and festivals offer excellent picture-taking possibilities. Select a spot with a clear view along the route, or if possible, from a slightly higher vantage. Try to get your friends and family in these shots by having them interact with costumed participants or those included in the parade.

An important tip to remember when visiting zoos and aquariums: Steer clear of taking too many pictures of dolphins performing in water shows. It's tempting, but if you don't keep the picture-taking to a minimum, you're going to come home with rolls of pictures featuring marine mammals, and very few of your friends or family and their reactions to their experiences. The same goes for shots of fireworks. Because of the darkness, the photos may not develop properly and you'll just have a bunch of black photos with distant fireworks. Instead, enjoy the fireworks from in front of the camera.

Self-timers are a must when traveling with friends and family! With self-timed photos, you can have pictures of your vacation that actually include you. This is especially important if you're honeymooning. How sad it is to flip through your honeymoon photo album and have barely any shots of you and your newlywed together!

One final tip—a rule that all professional photographers follow—is to simplify your subject by focusing on it, rather than on its surroundings. For example, imagine a shot of your children having a conversation with the Golden Gate Bridge in the background, rather than a shot of just the bridge itself. For more dramatic shots, be patient and wait for that perfect moment, or search for that unusual object. Focus and snap away—you'll find that the results will be most compelling!

67.
Together 24/7

It isn't until your very first vacation as an adult—whether taken on your honeymoon or with your family—that you come to the realization that you're going to be spending every day, all day, with the same people—sometimes for an entire week at a time.

So how do you do it without wanting to kill one another when it's over? Simple. Travelers must learn the number-one rule of traveling with others: respect.

When we respect our travel companions, we share with them the sense that we care about their feelings, their needs, and their desires. We learn to distinguish between when it's time to join them and when it's time to leave them alone. Respecting our travel companions' need for some privacy is one of the most considerate things we can do.

Respect works best if it's mutual, and it goes without saying that traveling companions need to support each other and be considerate of each other's feelings if a successful vacation together is to be had. There are many things that can become unbearable between even the closest of relations when spending extended time in such close quarters.

A perfect solution to avoid getting on each other's nerves during a vacation is to schedule some time every day, or every other day, apart. Whether it's a separate shopping hour, separate morning jogging times, visiting different sights, or a meal apart every day, the time spent away from each other builds excitement for the moment that you reunite and share your experiences with one another.

68.

Just the Two of Us

Just as time alone is important to honeymooners and families on vacation, it's equally important for those tired souls known as parents who are on a week's vacation with their kids. You'll have to make plans well in advance of your trip, but it is possible to find childcare while on vacation and guarantee yourself a few private hours.

In recent years, in an effort to lure more families to travel and vacation at their hotels and resorts, many fine establishments have begun catering specifically to the vacationing family. Research shows us that the number-one perk that parents look for in a resort or hotel is reliable, trustworthy evening care for their children so that they may steal away for dinner. Many hotels and resorts have answered this call, providing day and night camp for their younger guests and excellent, one-on-one baby-sitting service at night.

The same is true for locations abroad, provided your stay is in a big city or a popular vacation destination. Top hotels and resorts screen every baby-sitter who works for them and perform extensive background checks on their employees. Some hotels only hire teachers, daycare providers, and counselors by profession.

If you're apprehensive about leaving your children, but you're in desperate need of some time alone with your spouse while away, consider hiring a hotel sitter an hour or two earlier, to join the kids for dinner or to go out for some nearby sightseeing. This will give you and your children a chance to get to know the sitter, and you won't feel so uncomfortable about leaving them alone.

Your children may love their hotel baby-sitter. Why not let them enjoy this exciting experience? They'll have a ball playing games, snacking, and watching movies with someone new, and you can have fun with your spouse—even if it's just an escape to the hotel lobby for coffee!

69.

How to Screen the
Hotel Baby-Sitter

What often happens on vacation is that we tend to live our lives differently from the way that we live them at home. Everything changes when we're away from home—from the way that we eat to the way that we drive. But something we must never change—vacation or not—is our baby-sitter screening process. Think about it: You would never leave your children home at night with a person that you've never met before. Why would you agree to that just because you're on vacation?

However, performing a background check on a hotel baby-sitter is almost impossible. You have to trust that the hotel has prescreened all of their childcare employees using similar methods to those that you would use yourself. And most hotels do—especially the finer hotels and resorts.

You still need to take the screening process one step further. Vacationing parents should request a meeting earlier in the day with the sitter that the hotel has in mind to send you for that night. Introduce the sitter to your children—as you would were you back home—and see how they interact together. Ask the sitter how he would respond in an emergency, or what she would do in case of a fire. Does he know CPR? Is she familiar with local emergency numbers? Be sure to leave your sitter with a list of phone numbers where you can be reached (the restaurant that you'll be going to, for example). Let the sitter know that you can be called, no matter what—there's no such thing as a dumb question when your children's well-being is at stake.

Spend a good deal of time with the sitter before leaving the hotel. Ask him to take your kids for a short walk around the hotel to see how they'll get along alone. Or ask her to join you for lunch or dinner—this will give everyone the chance to become comfortable with one another and make the act of leaving a lot easier. If you have very young kids, give them ample time to get to know and trust the sitter before leaving—especially if your children tend to suffer from separation anxiety.

Most important, remember that you do not have to hire the baby-sitter that the hotel sends you. If you're unhappy or uncomfortable in the least, request that they send you somebody else. You need peace of mind that your children are content and safe while you're out—especially while you're in unfamiliar territory.

70.

Festival Occasions

Whether you're an experienced traveler seeking adventure or a beginner in search of some local flavor and color, visiting a world-famous festival may be just the thing to satisfy your craving! From Pamplona, Spain, to New Orleans, Louisiana, some of the larger festivals that the world has to offer provide a little something for everyone.

Do your research before you leave home. You may find that a location that you are visiting just happens to be known for an exciting annual festival. The experience can add a lot to your vacation.

Once you decide where you'll be vacationing, visit that destination's Chamber of Commerce online for a calendar of events, to find out if there are any festivals occurring while you're there. Or look online for a festival that interests you, and then head there for your vacation.

Know in advance, however, that lodging will be most expensive at all area hotels during the time of a popular festival. Perhaps you can consider staying near where the festival is taking place for a much better rate.

There's Mardi Gras in New Orleans in February or March for fun nights and days, complete with elaborate parades and plenty of rowdy behavior. If quiet, serene beauty is more your thing, why not head to Ottawa, Canada, in May for the Tulip Festival? The largest tulip festival in the world features five million tulips in arrangements created by twenty international floral designers.

For summer fun, you can attend the Running of the Bulls in Spain; watch the largest annual sporting event in the world, bicycling's Tour de France, in France; or head to Newport, Rhode Island, for their start-of-the-summer jazz festival. You can also end your summer with a trip to London to check out the largest street party in Europe, the Notting Hill Carnival. It features steel drum bands, elaborate costumes—and two million people! In the fall, the big deal is over in Munich, Germany, during Oktoberfest—6.5 million visitors eat German food, ride fair rides, and, of course, drink Masskrugs—one-liter mugs of beer.

Wherever you decide to be festive, you'll be thrilled to find out just how much fun a local festival can add to your vacation experience. Sample the local fare and mingle with the local residents —you just may end up coming back year after year!

71.

Time-Sharing

When parents select a vacation destination for the family, they are often hit with the difficult task of making sure that the trip offers a little something for each of their kids. It's wonderful to encourage each of your children to pursue his or her interests at home, but planning a family vacation around each individual's needs defeats the purpose. To ensure a "family" trip where each member participates in activities of general interest to all, follow these steps.

First, travel to a place where none of the sports or activities that your children excel in at home are offered! Instead, take them someplace where they can each experience new and different activities.

Rotate your children's interests. If one child loves tennis, but does not play on a regular basis, then go to a resort where tennis is offered. On the next trip, make sure to head to a place where your other child can ice skate and ski. Finally—and this is your best bet—search for a place that offers activities that all of your children enjoy. A travel agent can help you find the perfect place.

Remember this, too. Your desire to find this vacation utopia in order to satisfy your kids should not come at your expense! Take a good, hard look at your intentions. Are you trying to enrich your children's abilities, or just hoping to avoid hearing complaints and dissatisfaction? It's important to consider your children's interests, of course, but better to pick a vacation spot that you'll all enjoy, keeping in mind that you can't control their emotional reactions to new things.

Should one of your kids express unhappiness, don't ignore the disconnected child, but resist "rescuing" him or her from these temporary feelings. The experts tell us that children who manage to make the most of an unhappy situation emerge emotionally stronger. Don't set your kids up for vacation disappointment, of course, but when it happens, don't protect them from it, either!

72.

It's All Relative

There's nothing more exciting, more memorable—and more chaotic—than a big family reunion! Sure, you may be remembering family reunions from your childhood, where everyone always laughed a lot, had tremendous fun, and ate way too much food. What you don't remember, however, was the complete chaos that your parents went through orchestrating the event!

It can be scary to plan an event for a large group of people, but planning your extended family reunion can also be a rewarding, memorable experience that you will always cherish. The key is to approach the planning as you would any vacation—even if you and your immediate family won't be doing any traveling.

Decide well in advance what the event will be like, and then break the planning down into smaller steps. The most crucial part of planning a reunion is your guest list. Determining the number of guests will help determine what type of an event you can afford and where you will have it. Think carefully over your guest list—make sure that you include new spouses and children that you may not even know. Round up on your total: You will almost always have more relatives than you initially think!

Maybe you're lucky enough to have a huge backyard with a gigantic pool and a sports court. But what if you don't? You can still plan an amazing reunion chock-full of activities. Your choices include reserving space at a local park or campsite, or renting out a restaurant or catering hall. Still another option is to hold your reunion at an all-inclusive, family-friendly spot. Many dude ranches, hotel resorts, and cruises offer all meals, lodging, and activities included — and many of them offer excellent rates for large groups.

Your decision all boils down to one thing: money. If you decide to host your family reunion aboard a cruise ship or at an all-inclusive resort, consider how much money you are willing to spend and how much money your guests will be willing to spend. Whatever your plans, be sure that your guests are clear about who's paying. If it's going to be you, let them know. If you're just securing rooms for them and don't intend to foot the bill, make sure they know that, too.

Next, do your homework. Do your plans include activities for everyone? The difficult part about large families is finding stimulating, fun activities for the young and old alike. Make sure there is plenty for everyone to do every day.

You will have to prepare yourself for a few unhappy reunion guests. You can't please everyone! Relax and remember the reason that you got everyone together in the first place — to celebrate your family and to get closer to the people that you call relatives.

73.

Functioning Without the Minivan

Back home, in your everyday life, your vehicle functions as more than just a mode of transportation. It is, in fact, an extension of your home. When you're away on vacation and forced to use a foreign, unfamiliar vehicle, only then do you develop a true appreciation of your car, minivan, or SUV back home. How can you possibly function without it?

Rest assured, even the most car-dependent travelers can learn to make do with a rental car or with public transportation. What it means, for the most part, is going on vacation prepared with yet one more backpack. In addition to the carry-on backpack that you have for the plane ride, the kids' activity packs for combating boredom, and the day pack that you need for a successful vacation, if you plan on renting a car while you're on vacation, you'll need to assemble the rental car pack. If it sounds cumbersome, just think what it will be like when you're trapped at a scenic overlook along the highway with three children and no toilet paper.

Toilet paper is an essential part of your rental car backpack. Bottled water is another key element. Take as many bottles as you can fit—the water will be imperative in an emergency, for keeping things and children clean, and for quenching thirst. Don't be tempted to take carbonated water or fruit-flavored water, since you may not need it for drinking.

First-aid supplies, matches, paper towels, extra sweatshirts for everyone, a towel (you never know), rain ponchos, wipes, antibacterial soap, and emergency candy or snacks can all be stuffed into your rental car backpack. Remember that you will not be carrying this pack around, so don't worry about overstuffing it. It will remain in the car throughout your trip. You don't need to include car safety items, but make sure that your car's trunk is equipped with the safety supplies that you'll need should you encounter an emergency—flares, wiper fluid, and oil, to name a few. Armed with the essentials that you're used to having handy at all times during your everyday life will make your vacation days run that much better.

74.

Driving in a Foreign Country

Even if you're an impeccable driver with years of experience, if you plan on getting behind the wheel while on vacation, there are several matters you'll want to keep in mind to ensure your safety and the safety of your passengers. Driving in Europe is not the same as driving in the United States. Nearly everything is different about driving in a foreign country, including the side of the road driven on, the mechanical differences in foreign cars, and even drivers' hand gestures.

Since you have no way of knowing the driving customs of the particular country that you are in, before you slip the key into the ignition of your rental, ask the clerk at the rental company for some driving tips and pointers. Ask about right-on-red and right-of-way rules, ask if your car has antilock brakes, ask for a quick lesson on road signs, and ask if there are any important hand signals that you need to know to get by.

Before driving off the rental lot, ask if your car is equipped with driver or dual air bags. Never let children under the age of twelve ride in the front passenger seat anyway, but definitely not if there is a passenger-side airbag.

Drive defensively, no matter what country you are in. Prevent accidents or road rage by avoiding bully motorists and traffic crunches, especially in crowded areas. If you are bumped by another driver, or should he or she attempt to make you pull over, keep driving until you reach a well-populated, well-lit area. Then you can check out the situation.

Ask the rental agency for a car without agency decals or other distinguishing marks that identify it as a rental car. It's never a good idea to advertise the fact that you're an out-of-towner. Keep all maps under the seats when you leave the car unattended, and store all valuables—and your car rental pack—in the trunk, out of sight. Keep all doors and windows closed and locked when you park, and bring all valuables into your hotel room with you at night.

Finally, make sure that your car is equipped with safety items such as flares, jumper cables, a flashlight, a first-aid kit, and wiper fluid. If your car starts overheating, it can help if you turn on your heater. This draws heat away from your engine and may help you make it safely to the nearest garage or gas station.

The extra key is the absolute essential item for minimizing your vacation car rental anxiety. It's very easy to leave the keys in a rental car because you're not used to the routine of driving this particular car. Be prepared by carrying an extra key in your pocket, shoe, or money belt, and avoid a catastrophe!

75.

Away from Homeland Security

According to the U.S. State Department, there are many potential threats against American tourists at any given time. Because of this, U.S. government facilities around the world are on heightened alert at all times.

There's no need to become overly alarmed if you're planning a trip abroad. Safety involves using common sense and following some basic rules. Most important, travelers need to exercise vigilance and increase their security awareness to reduce their vulnerability to danger. The State Department (www.state.gov/travel) issues many safety suggestions to keep yourself secure on vacation—if you're planning a trip abroad, visit their web site to familiarize yourself with all of their warnings. Keep in mind that the State Department issues advisories of several different kinds—not just terrorist advisories. Carefully check the advisory (if there is one) for your destination.

In addition, many Internet services offer visitors news and alerts of breaking situations and changes in travel conditions. If you're overly cautious, you can find some services on the web that offer (for a fee) a "personal guardian" service that includes a cell phone, 24/7 itinerary monitoring, real-time travel alerts, and around-the-clock travel and medical assistance while you're away.

The most important thing that you can do to ensure your safety while on vacation is to keep a low profile. The State Department offers this tip: Vary your travel route. Heading on and off the beaten path can be just the way to avoid threats to your safety. Try not to be so predictable in your itinerary—change the routes that you take, the restaurants that you visit, and the stores where you shop.

Be on the lookout for suspicious objects—unattended bags or suitcases at airports, packages left on park benches—and never accept anything from strangers. Most difficult will be keeping an eye on your rental car. Try to park it in a garage rather than on the street where somebody can tamper with it.

Finally, keep your sense of humor and let yourself enjoy your vacation! While there's nothing humorous about political strife, there's something comical about getting so worked up over the *possibility* of violence that you spend your precious vacation days wearing a bulletproof vest along with your bathing suit.

76.

First-Aid on the Go

Keeping healthy on the road can make or break any trip. Smart travelers should be equipped with a first-aid kit—either in their day pack or rental car. The contents and size of your kit depend on how you'll be traveling (on foot, by car, or by public transportation) and where you're going. If you're visiting a city, your kit can be smaller, since there are likely to be pharmacies nearby. If you're backpacking or going on a camping trip or outdoor adventure to a remote location, you'll need to be prepared for additional minor traumas.

Take only what you think you'll need, and small amounts of it. Leave the bottles of pills at home (unless, of course, you'll need a large supply), and consider purchasing a plastic pill carrier with several compartments. This way, you can bring along a few different medications and keep them from getting mixed up. Most important, remember to label the pill carrier covers!

Choose your drugs wisely—over-the counter pills can often be used to treat more than one ailment. Antihistamines, for example, treat allergies, but can also work to make you drowsy if you need to sleep. Consider taking both ibuprofen and acetaminophen, since ibuprofen can be bothersome to your stomach—something you don't need while on vacation.

Basically, your first-aid travel kit should contain an antibiotic ointment to topically treat abrasions and prevent infection, and an antiseptic for cleaning cuts and scrapes. Individually wrapped wipes are perfect for fitting into a small kit. Include plenty of adhesive bandages, some calamine lotion, and lip balm for dry lips. Many travelers tend to buy new shoes before going on vacation, so it's also a good idea to have a blister kit. Include a rehydration solution (sugar and water) to treat dehydration. Finally, scissors, tweezers, and a thermometer should be included for general health issues. (Make sure that you don't bring a mercury thermometer, as they are prohibited by the airlines.) Traveling to the tropics may require some additional first-aid items like insect bite treatments, antidiarrheal, and malaria prophylaxis, plus water purification tablets if you're unsure about the condition of the water where you'll be staying.

Luckily, the pharmaceutical companies have answered the needs of travelers and created smaller versions of many of these medications. Many even offer prefabricated first-aid kits—if assembling one on your own seems like a hassle, don't leave town before purchasing one ready to go!

77.

Are You Prepared
for an Emergency?

Unfortunately, many vacationers are faced with emergency situations during the course of their trips. What usually helps them get through any highly troublesome times is the preparations that they made before leaving home.

When your first-aid kit simply won't cut it and you need medical attention while abroad, your first move should be to contact the American consulate or embassy (or the Canadian, British, Irish, or Australian consulates) to find the name of a reliable, English-speaking physician. American hospitals, large government-run hospitals, and missionary clinics are likely to have good physicians as well. If it's medical attention of the most serious nature that you seek, the State Department's Overseas Citizens Emergency Center in Washington, D.C., is the place to call. They can notify relatives of your problems, help wire money, and expedite the transfer of medical information.

Before leaving for vacation, make a list of your physicians and their emergency phone numbers, with country and city codes included in the numbers. Include the phone number for the State Department, and the number of the International Association for Medical Assistance to Travelers (IAMAT). They will be able to provide you with information on English-speaking physicians.

If you're staying at a large hotel, chances are that the hotel staff will have a list of physicians and pharmacies available. Be aware of foreign medications that are prescribed for you, however. Some drugs sold overseas are unsafe for people of Anglo-Saxon descent. Aminopyrine, for example, which is sold as an analgesic in Japan, is one such drug.

Should you find yourself receiving care in a foreign hospital, ask your travel companions to investigate the fees involved. Many European health care facilities don't charge anything, and some charge high fees. You should be able to pay a hospital with your credit card.

It helps to avoid further potential problems abroad by understanding your own personal insurance policy before traveling. Some policies have geographic restrictions. Others won't cover you at all out of the United States. Call your carrier beforehand to determine whether or not you should purchase additional insurance, such as an emergency assistance plan. Other numbers and things to assemble before leaving home include the number for the American consulate where you'll be staying, your bank account numbers and PIN number, a telephone calling card account and number, and a contact at Western Union.

Should you get arrested while on vacation, contact the nearest American consulate for an advocate familiar with the customs and procedures of the country, and should you be the victim of a violent or nonviolent crime, report it to the police immediately. Your insurance company will not reimburse you otherwise.

Try to remain as calm as possible in an emergency overseas. The language barrier, the country's unfamiliar procedures, and many other factors are likely to confuse you—panicking can only make the situation worse! Keep in mind that if you have your passport, access to your money, and the phone number of an English-speaking contact, you can get through most emergencies abroad.

78.

Indulge in
Room Service

L ooking to treat yourself to one of life's greatest vacation luxuries? It's there in your hotel room, right at your fingertips. It's the room service menu!

There's something decadent about room service—even if it just involves ordering a pizza for your hungry family. Somebody else takes care of the details involved in feeding your family, while you do something different—or nothing at all.

One factor to remember about room service—and try not to let this diminish your excitement over ordering it—is the fact that your bill may end up higher than you expected. One travel expert points out that vacationers must always carefully scrutinize their room service bills to identify what they are paying for. Many hotels impose a "gratuity" charge—between fifteen and eighteen percent—which means that you do not have to add another tip. It may be nice to leave your server something extra, but the bulk of the tip is already included. Vacations are the perfect time to take advantage of life's little pleasures, and if that means indulging yourself in the convenience of tasty, hot food arriving magically at your door, then so be it! For many, this little extravagance is all part of the total vacation experience.

79.

Here's a Tip…

American travelers were polled by a travel magazine in early 2000 and asked for the number-one most stressful thing about vacationing. Surprisingly, tipping ranked very high on the list. Tipping philosophies are so different from country to country and culture to culture that giving too much or not giving enough becomes a source of anxiety for many travelers. While many of us consider a tip something to be earned, there are specific guidelines to help you decide on an appropriate gratuity for all of those hardworking employees who provide services to you during a trip.

Tipping in Europe isn't very different than in the States—waiters, hotel staff, and taxi drivers expect about the same kind of compensation as their American counterparts. One difference, however, is that in Europe, service charges are often included in the bills at most hotels and restaurants. If they are, no additional tipping is necessary—but always ask, regardless, so as not to slight any servicepeople.

Tipping in the Mideast and Africa differs so substantially from country to country that the only way to know how much to tip is to check a guidebook under "tipping" for each country that you plan on visiting.

As for tipping in Asia and Australia, the subject is taken very personally. In China and Australia, generally nobody tips. In China, actually, it's considered insulting to offer a tip! In Australia, only waiters in the finest restaurants expect a ten percent tip. Taxi drivers in Australia do not expect tips, but it's common practice to round up to the nearest Australian dollar when paying. Tipping and service charges are nonexistent in New Zealand.

Other Asian countries have drastically different tipping policies. In Japan, tipping is never expected. If you still wish to offer something extra, you should do so by sealing your tip in a decorative, sealed envelope and formally presenting it as a gift. In parts of Vietnam, tipping is outlawed but discreetly practiced in restaurants!

It's a good idea to research tipping policies in the country where you're headed. Then you can ensure getting terrific service and hospitality abroad, and you won't find yourself distressed over whether you've left too much or too little.

80.

Understanding
the Locals

While your main priority when traveling in unfamiliar territory should always be safety, it will really spice up your trip if you can mingle a little with the locals and experience their culture. If your plans call for travel to unfamiliar lands, do your homework before you leave, and gain a little insight into the local customs. This is especially helpful if you're traveling alone or if you are female. Additional knowledge can help you stay alert while you explore and increase your enjoyment and safety.

Despite the stereotype of the "ugly American," most people do want to meet Americans! You'll find out the most information about a new culture from local teenagers, who are often fascinated by American pop culture. (In many cases, young people have knowledge of English from school or picked up from movies and television.) Bring along a small collection of American items to use for gifts if you're headed to a foreign country.

For recreation, do as the locals do! Go to soccer matches, flea markets, fairs, and festivals. Don't bother with the touristy nightclubs and pubs listed in your travel guide—instead, hit a few local pubs for the most authentic experience.

Again, use common sense. Women should take note of the behavior and dress of the local women. Women who travel alone are often assumed to be open to making new acquaintances. It's a good idea to indicate that you are not open to this at all if you're approached by anyone who makes you feel uncomfortable. Better yet, learn the word "no" in the local language.

The common sense that you apply to situations back home should still hold true when traveling abroad and immersing yourself in a new culture. Avoid dimly lit areas, walk with confidence, and be aware of what's going on around you at all times. Stay in crowded areas, and if you're a woman who finds herself in a compromising situation, seek help from other women.

If you find that you constantly meet the same English-speaking tourists over and over, it means that you are probably following the same guidebook. Go ahead and make friends with these people—they obviously have the same tastes and traveling style as you—and together you can visit those interesting local places. You'll do so in a much safer atmosphere.

81.

Have Fun!

There are so many rules to remember when vacationing — rules about safety, dining, hotel stays, keeping children entertained, transportation — it can sometimes be hard to remember to have fun as well! The next time that you slip into vacation mode, try repeating this to yourself every morning: "Remember to have fun! Remember to have fun!"

There are plenty of ways that travelers can achieve the most joy from their travel experiences. But it's sometimes the smallest changes to your vacation routine that offer other happy surprises. Waking up early, for example, can be something simple that you can do to have fun on your vacation. If you're traveling with small children, the predawn hours may be the only time that you'll find any alone time. Ask your spouse to help the kids with their morning routines so that you can enjoy your morning cup of coffee at an attraction that you've been waiting to see. Some places are best when experienced at daybreak. At dawn, chances are that you won't be sharing them with very many other tourists!

Being flexible with your choice of transportation can provide added vacation pleasures. Walking is the best choice. It can give you the flavor of a place better than anything. The sights, sounds, and smells of the city or countryside are better experienced when you're not enclosed in a vehicle. You might try renting a bicycle for a day to enjoy the sights as you pedal through town. Try horseback or camel riding, destination permitting, or see the sights of a city in a boat along the river. Hike through mountains and countryside to enjoy what a getaway truly has to offer. Most important, be spontaneous. Keep track of where you are, but don't resist walking down that narrow, winding road if it catches your eye.

Bring your camera or journal with you every day to record your experiences. Don't deny yourself the pleasures that you've been dreaming about—even if it means lugging around an easel and a palette of oil paints everywhere you go!

82.

The Art of
Shopping on Vacation

Whatever it is that you might be buying, most street vendors around the world expect to do a little haggling before parting with their wares. Unfortunately, they've become quite good at it. Do your homework and stick to your guns when it comes to haggling in a foreign country. Live by the golden rule of negotiation: You can always walk away! Make sure that you follow that rule if your haggling goes nowhere.

At the start of your vacation, use the first few days for looking, not buying. Get a feel for the merchandise and scope out the highest quality products. Ask fellow souvenir shoppers what the going rates are for your favorite items, and use that as a benchmark. Later, when you're ready to spend, you'll have more realistic starting prices.

When you are ready to buy, make sure that you are familiar with the local currency. You're less likely to be conned if you can read the prices correctly and make change by yourself. Carry small denominations of currency so that you can pay closer to the exact haggled-upon price. It's common for vendors to pretend that they don't have change! It's also a common practice for them to give you dirty or torn bills as change—bills that they know no other merchant will accept. Don't accept them, either.

Watch how you dress for a day of haggling. Vendors are not going to budge on their price if they think that you have a lot of money to spend. Plus, avoid approaching a store or shop proclaiming your desperate desire to have what they're selling.

Finally, you have what you want in hand, and you're ready to haggle. Once you've declared that you're not sure you want the item, make an offer of half the asking price. Of course, the vendor will appear shocked and offended, but no matter how much he or she insists that the product is worth twice that, remain firm.

Resist the urge to pay full price! Even if you absolutely must have the item, you need to keep the upper hand in the negotiations. If the bargaining comes to a deadlock and you aren't happy with the price, thank the vendor and leave the store. A serious seller will follow you out and offer you a better price.

83.

Take a Vacation from Your Vacation

If you and your loved ones are doing your best, but clearly not enjoying your vacation, it is possible to change your plans. Depending on where you are, most vacation destinations are close to other vacation destinations. If you're in Europe, other cities are just a train ride away. In the islands, other resorts are also close by and easily accessible. If you're not having the time of your life on vacation, it may pay to spend an hour or so investigating an emergency vacation change.

Start by calling other hotels or resorts to check on their availability, and then call the airlines to see what the penalty is for changing flights (often, it's minimal). Or simply head down to the hotel lobby and ask to speak to the manager. Explain your discontent and ask for advice. He or she may be able to direct you to another, more appropriate destination—or if there is another hotel in the same chain somewhere else, transfer your reservation for the remainder of your trip.

Often, people remain on a mediocre vacation purely out of convenience. It does take legwork to turn your vacation plans around, not to mention repacking and unpacking—but travelers do it all the time. Look at it this way: If this is your one week away a year, why would you settle for mediocrity? Put in the extra effort, and get your vacation going the way that you hoped it would go! So what if there are only four days left of your vacation week? Isn't it worth spending those last four days having fun instead of just making the best of it?

84.

Rules for Parents

Vacation days can be long ones. Earnest moms and dads have worn themselves out exposing their kids to culture and fun, often at the expense of their own vacation rest. It helps to remember that when you're on vacation, there are "vacation rules." The policies that you stick to at home don't necessarily translate while you're away.

The number-one vacation rule for parents is that if you need to rest, let them watch TV. This will probably come up early in the morning or late in the afternoon when everyone needs a break. If TV is not an option in your hotel room, try one of these suggestions.

Have a scavenger hunt. You can hide small items or pennies around the room and have your kids make a game out of finding them. The more that you hide, the longer that you'll get to nap! You can also have them hide the objects from each other and take turns finding them.

Color postcards. Prepare postcard-sized oak tag rectangles, and let your children color their own postcards of places that they've seen. Then address them and mail them from the lobby.

Have them play games. Many hotels have board games, cards, checkers, chess, and backgammon for guests to take to their rooms. If your children are too young for these games, borrow them anyway — children are usually imaginative enough to make their own games up using the pieces.

Finally, make a deal with your spouse. Take a one-hour nap while your spouse entertains the children — preferably out of the room — and then reciprocate by taking the kids somewhere for an hour so that he or she can nap. Explore the hotel, go for ice cream, or just sit in the lobby and people-watch!

85.

Writing It
All Down

For many travelers, cameras, video cameras, and souvenirs are absolute musts for capturing a vacation's most memorable moments. For others, recording the events of a vacation in a journal is more their style.

What you write in your vacation journal depends a lot on who you are writing for. If you're keeping a journal for yourself, you can jot down more personal information—thoughts, ideas, and dreams that you experience while visiting new places and meeting new people. If your journal is intended as a keepsake for your children or for your family, it helps to organize your pages in scrapbook form.

A vacation scrapbook will become a great souvenir for many years to come. While traveling, take time to jot down the events and fun times that you want to remember. Get started the moment that a thought hits you—reach for your journal and pen and write! Remember to leave room for photographs that can be pasted in later.

The key to successful journal-writing is recording the who, what, why, when, and where of your day—not necessarily in that order. Be sure to first record the place, the time, and the date of your experience, since you'll drive yourself crazy later on trying to remember when you visited! Begin your entry with why you decided to visit the particular location and a few facts about it.

When you have all the necessary facts recorded, it's time to get creative! Take in the surroundings, capturing the scenery in descriptive adjectives. Think about your reaction to the place and how it differs from how you thought you'd react. If your children and spouse are with you, pay attention to their reactions, as well, and record what you see and hear. Ask them questions about what they're experiencing, and fill your pages with their quotes.

Finally, let your thoughts and ideas speak for themselves. There's no need to embellish, especially if you'll be adding photographs later. When you travel, collect brochures of each place along the way—they can also make a great addition to your prose! Don't shy away from being poetic—even if you've never written poetry before. Let the scenery, the experience, and the moment inspire you, and you'll have the makings of a journal to keep forever.

86.

Put Down the Video Camera

Video cameras are wonderful things, especially on family vacations, where there is usually no shortage of subjects to film. If you are the designated videographer, however, be careful that while filming, you don't miss out on any precious moments and occurrences going on around you. For many, entire vacations are seen through that viewfinder instead of appreciated through the use of one's full senses.

Be selective when filming. Work to capture interesting snippets of your subjects candidly, rather than having them pose for the camera. People always feel so stupid when that red light comes on and taping begins—they never know what to do! They'll wave for a few seconds, and then usually ask outright (and this is always caught on tape), "Can we stop waving now?"

If you decide to bring your video camera on your next vacation, make sure that you're aware of how much you're actually filming. Time yourself, if you must, to ensure that you don't spend the whole day filming memories instead of making them.

87.

Unconventional Souvenirs

The great thing about vacation souvenirs is that sometimes, the tackier the item, the better a souvenir it makes! The best thing about souvenirs is their tackiness—how else could one explain the incredible popularity of snow globes, dashboard hula dancers, or "My grandparents went to…" T-shirts?

Our desire for souvenirs while vacationing is twofold. We consume them up for their kitsch quality, to put on a shelf or in a drawer somewhere to remind us of the fun that we had visiting a certain place. Also, we're always expected to bring home gifts for our friends and relatives. The generally low prices of souvenirs make this especially easy when buying in bulk.

Purchasing souvenirs can become quite a burden. Include only the people that you absolutely must bring things home for—don't stray from that list, or you'll find yourself overloaded and broke.

Vacation souvenirs don't always have to be in the form of cheap, plastic mementos scooped up at a souvenir shop along the highway. You can bring home interesting gifts for others from your trip by thinking creatively rather than digging into your wallet.

Postcards make terrific souvenirs—and they're usually pretty inexpensive. Stock up on postcards depicting places that you've visited, and then create gift packs of ten different cards for each friend or family member back home. During free time on your trip, write something about the place depicted for each person. You'll have a little personal scrapbook to give to everyone by the time that you're through.

Memory glasses make fun, entertaining souvenirs, too. Inside a small jar, place collectible items like foreign coins, railway tokens, small pictures, or sand and seashells from the beaches that you visited. Create a colorful label, and write something that you remember about the site on it, and then seal the jar closed.

Other souvenir ideas include poems, homemade videos, personalized photographs of yourself at a landmark, or—a favorite inexpensive souvenir item—stamps. Stamps are especially fun if you're planning on visiting a few different countries. For just a dollar or two, you can purchase many differently designed stamps and have a ready-made collection to give to your friends back home.

88.

Lugging Luggage That You Like

If you don't have excellent luggage for your vacation, don't bother going. The reason is that if you're going on vacation to get away from the hassles, problems, and stress of everyday life, going with luggage that is flimsy, cheap, or too heavy is going to create more hassles, problems, and stress for you!

Choose your luggage wisely. While expensive leather cases may look and feel fabulous, they cost a fortune and can become damaged by baggage handlers on your very first trip. Durability is the key word when shopping for luggage.

Many travelers often return home from a vacation with a lot more than they left with. Expandable, soft-sided luggage is a great choice if you'll be buying souvenirs and other things on your trip. Hard-sided luggage is durable, and it's a good idea only if you think that you'll be bringing home very delicate items.

Having wheels on your luggage is of great importance! Bags with wheels are convenient and can save your back, arm, shoulder, and neck muscles from a lot of undue stress.

Luggage that locks discourages would-be thieves. However, with today's stricter airport laws, you must be prepared to make the key readily available, or security will have to break the locks to check your bags.

Consider luggage with plenty of compartments. Expandable pockets on the outside work best (especially for transporting toiletries), and they don't take up inside space.

Finally, if you're purchasing a set of luggage, go with a bright color or pattern. This can make your bags more easily distinguishable from all of the other brown, navy, and black sets that make their way around the conveyor belts. Spotting your bags early on can save you lots of stressful time at the airport.

89.
To Go or
Not to Go?

If the thought of danger while traveling causes you great anxiety, you might be better off staying home and finding activities nearby that you can enjoy instead. But before you decide to abandon the plans for the vacation that you've been saving for, become an informed American. The U.S. State Department can give you information regarding travel advisories that may make you feel more comfortable about vacationing at your destination.

Increased air and rail security has contributed to consumer confidence. Customers must show a photo ID when buying tickets and checking luggage—and they can no longer purchase tickets aboard some trains. In this country, airlines and rail companies have internal police forces that are now a more visible presence, and they work closely with the FBI to prevent possibly threatening situations from coming to fruition. In other countries, railroad security has changed, too. There are more police, trash cans in terminals have been replaced with transparent plastic bags, and self-service luggage lockers have been eliminated.

At many hotels all over the world, security measures have been stepped up. Guests are often required to present ID at check-in and show their room keys when parking or boarding elevators. Property entrances may be guarded around the clock or surveillance systems may be installed.

The government and airlines are working to share information to restore public confidence, and our aviation security system is rapidly changing. Bags, shoes, carry-ons, cargo, and even people are now all routinely screened.

Traveling *is* risky, but so is walking across the street of your hometown. The important thing to remember when making a decision about whether or not to leave home is that there are precautions in place to protect you.

90.

Stress in the Sky

As unfortunate as it is, in addition to anxiety caused by the threat of terrorism, airplane mechanical problems, and a general fear of flying, air travelers have yet another reason to feel anxious: air rage. Recently, air rage has become so extreme that travelers have even been subject to passengers assaulting flight attendants, behaving obscenely, and making completely irrational decisions that affect the safety of their fellow passengers on board.

The reasons for air rage are easy to understand. With fewer flights and more people crammed onto planes with extremely tight space, people feel trapped, confined, and claustrophobic. Add into the mix the usual restrictions that passengers are forced to follow, like staying in their seats with their belts buckled, and you have the makings of a hostile environment. Alcohol also contributes to this problem—nearly all passengers who experience one form or another of air rage are found to be inebriated.

If you're traveling with people who are prone to rage or high-strung by nature, discourage them from drinking, or keep them occupied with conversation, the in-flight movie, or a book. If you know someone to be very volatile, you may even suggest that he or she take a mild sedative before flying. Under no circumstances should you intervene in the case of a passenger experiencing air rage, unless that passenger poses a threat to you, other passengers, or the plane itself.

Your airline staff has been trained extensively if a situation arises, so let them do their job. There is a set of handcuffs on all airplanes, and pilots are instructed to radio ahead for police to be in position upon landing. Standard procedure is that the plane be evacuated upon landing, with the perpetrator deplaned last so as to avoid any further incidents.

Air rage cannot be dismissed or excused. An assault on a flight attendant is a violation of federal law that carries a maximum sentence of twenty years in prison. Take heart in the fact that although the number of air rage incidents seems high, compared to the number of flights, it is actually very low.

91.

The Vacation Five

It happens to the best of us—even the most disciplined dieters who calorie count: When we go on vacation, we come home five pounds heavier than when we started out. It isn't hard to explain why. For the most part, when we're away from home, all food is fair game!

On vacation, we tend to throw caution to the wind. We're out for a good time, and we've paid a lot of money to have one. But here's the good news: You can enjoy the delicious, often sinful foods that other countries are famous for while on vacation and not return home one size larger. You just have to remember the two basic rules of dining on the road: Don't deny yourself anything, and share everything!

Make a deal with yourself beforehand that every day you'll allow yourself a culinary indulgence. This way, you know that you'll be sinking your teeth into something delicious at some point, and you can enjoy the whole day without wasting energy worrying about your diet. Choose the time that's right for you—a hearty breakfast, a five-course gourmet dinner, or a decadent dessert. This way, you'll get to sample what you came for, and you won't put on those extra pounds.

Make it a point to take a long walk every morning before you head out for the day. This bit of exercise will work wonders on those extra calories from the day before! You'll feel better during the rest of your vacation—and you'll look better when you get home.

92.

Surfside Safety

For the safest beach environment for you and your family, you should always opt for a patrolled beach with lifeguards stationed near the shoreline. Having professionals nearby for your safety lowers the risks involved in beach and underwater activities.

Should you decide to visit a less populated beach during your vacation, beware of the hidden dangers that exist. It stands to reason that everyone involved should be a strong swimmer. Avoiding alcohol, which can hamper your abilities and judgment, is extremely important.

Many different and dangerous kinds of bacteria thrive in seawater, and if ingested, they can make you sick. They can also invade your body through your eyes, nose, or ears, enter through cuts and other wounds, or affect your skin on contact.

Jellyfish and other sea creatures such as sea nettles, sea anemones, and sea wasps all have venomous stings. The venom, in the worst cases, can cause paralysis of the breathing muscles, and eventually death if resuscitation is not performed. The biggest, most deadly jellyfish can be found in Southeast Asia and Australia.

There are many underwater creatures to be aware of—so prepare yourself beforehand by researching the names of the most dangerous that populate the region that you'll be visiting. It goes without saying that if you're visiting beaches known for their shark or alligator populations, don't plan on swimming.

Make sure to keep away from coral in the interest of preserving it (touching or stepping on coral can kill it and it takes many years for coral to grow again), and because some species of coral can sting. Cone mollusks—a favorite among shell collectors—are also dangerous. A live cone can sting you with its tongue and cause paralysis, or even death.

The world's most dangerous underwater creature is the stonefish. It lies on the ocean floor, resembling a rock or a stone. It has highly poisonous spines down its back that can penetrate even thick-soled shoes, if jumped upon.

So follow some good advice and stick to the patrolled, lifeguarded beaches on vacation. If you simply must explore new, unpopulated shores, be sure to ask the locals about the creatures that inhabit their waters.

93.

Travel Fraud

Let the buyer beware! Even the travel industry is rampant with fraud. If you receive an offer for a vacation package in the mail or over the telephone that sounds too good to be true, then it usually is!

Always read the fine print in an offer that you find suspicious. Check all references and affiliated companies with the Better Business Bureau or with the Federal Trade Commission before you purchase anything. Most important, never give your credit card information to a company that you do not know or trust!

Some telemarketers will use any tactic possible to get you to buy into their pitch. Usually, they'll insist that you make a decision on the spot—that their amazing offer is good at that very moment only. These are the promotions that you should be wary about. You should always be given a chance to think about your purchase—if someone can't agree to call you back at another time (even if it's later that day), then it's reasonable to be suspicious. Many of these companies are on the up-and-up, but a good majority of them are also part of travel marketing schemes that bilk millions of dollars from consumers.

On the other hand, don't be so overly cautious that you pass up what might be a perfectly legitimate, unbelievable deal. There are plenty of travel deals to be had out there, and should you take advantage of one, you'll have yourself a fabulous vacation for a very small fee. Just be sure to exercise caution and investigate any and every company that calls you at home with one of those "spectacular vacation offers."

94.

The Hotel Stairmaster

If you're a fitness buff, you're probably familiar with vacation exercise already. Plenty of people who exercise regularly keep to their routines while on vacation. For the rest of us who perhaps aren't so dedicated, in general, vacation time presents the perfect opportunity to jump on the fitness bandwagon! There's something inspiring about going for a jog near the very places you came to visit for an exhilarating experience that can set the pace for a brand-new, healthy attitude.

Begin the new, healthier you by learning a few airplane exercises that can prepare you for vacation—and keep you comfortable for the ride. Research has indicated that at high altitudes, oxygen tension in the arteries decreases, leading to vasodilation and a greater risk of thrombosis and pulmonary embolism than while you're on the ground. That can cause swelling in your legs and ultimately blood clots—and perhaps even heart failure.

Frequent, rhythmic stretching in your seat, paying close attention to your legs and neck, can help reduce swelling. If you notice a sudden lull in aisle commotion, use it as an opportunity to bounce up and down on your toes, twist your torso, and take a walk down the aisle. Most important, keep yourself well-hydrated—avoiding caffeine and alcohol—to avoid further blood circulation problems.

Once you've arrived at your hotel, check out the fitness room. You really won't need much for a decent morning workout. If the fitness room is nonexistent, check to see what condition the pool is in and if it is open early in the morning. Walking and jogging may be an alternative. Some hotels can even provide you with a jogger's map—a carefully planned route around the hotel and vicinity—so that you won't get lost.

Should your hotel have a disappointing setup, you can always investigate other hotels or gyms in the area to see if they will let you use their facilities. As a last resort, there's always the chair in your hotel room—not for sitting in, but for use as an anchor so that you can do some light stretching and lifting.

95.

Winding Down

There's always an anxious feeling people get when they're at the tail end of a vacation—the feeling that they haven't seen everything that they'd hoped to see, or that they haven't found the perfect souvenirs. For this reason, many group tours include a "free day" at the end of the trip to provide vacationers with extra time to shop or an opportunity to return to a sight at which they'd hoped to spend more time. If you're traveling alone or with your family, you should do the same—be sure to include some scheduled free time.

Perhaps weather kept you from seeing a certain site that you had read about. If you've allowed yourselves a block of free time, you can use it to return to any places that you had really been looking forward to, but had to miss.

Winding down your vacation is also important if you anticipate beforehand the mixed emotions that you're sure to experience as you leave the place on which you've been focused for months! The trip that you've been planning for and dreaming about is almost over, and soon you'll be returning to normal life. Pace yourself accordingly as you near the end, to give yourself ample opportunity to let all of your experiences really soak in. Don't fall into the trap of ending your vacation two days early because you know that you'll be leaving soon—make the most out of every moment, right up until it's time to leave for the airport. Don't waste valuable vacation time packing, either—save that for the night before you leave. Many of us think packing to go home and checking out of the hotel are going to be very time-consuming, when really they don't take much time at all.

Savor your final vacation moments. It wouldn't hurt to save the most anticipated, exciting sights for the very end of your trip, either!

96.

The Night-Before Checklist

The night before your trip home can be a night filled with emotion, anxiety, and just plain chaos. Where do you begin? When you left for vacation, you had days — even weeks — to get ready, pack, and prepare. Now you have just a few short hours. But not to worry — it will all get done!

Before thinking about packing, take a few moments to prioritize the more important tasks that you need to accomplish, such as what you need to declare for customs. Customs officials at the airport check for two things: the dutiable items that you purchased abroad, and the items that you are not permitted to bring back into the country. Know that your luggage will be checked at the airport — sometimes more than once — so if you have something to declare, you ought to declare it.

Pack and organize your receipts so that they are readily available to present. Customs officials are professionals — they know the value of most everything! If they discover that you have undervalued

215

something, they will confiscate it and fine you its U.S. value. You're entitled to a personal exemption of four hundred dollars—with certain limitations—and purchases must be intended for personal use. It's wise to be informed of all customs rules and regulations before going to the airport. Duty-free items include diamonds (cut but not set), books, antiques produced more than one hundred years ago (you'll need proof of this), works of art, stamps, natural pearls, and exposed film. There is a fine line as to what constitutes a work of art, so it's best to ask for the details at the place where you purchased the art.

Don't offer to transport packages for others—you never know what could be inside. Most fruits, vegetables, meats, poultry, live animals, and hazardous articles are prohibited.

Once you have put aside your declared items, you can begin the packing process. For the most part, you're going to have dirty laundry—unless you've been cleaning your clothes at the hotel. Use your largest suitcase to pack dirty clothing only. Then repack your toiletries in plastic, and stuff them into the dirty-clothes suitcase.

Your other suitcase (if you have one) should be used for your remaining clean clothes and your breakable souvenirs that you don't need to declare. Use cotton clothing to wrap breakable items and pack them together in your smaller suitcase or carry-on bag.

That night, pack up absolutely everything—except for the clothes that you'll need for the trip home and the toiletries that you may need in the morning. The night before is also a good time to wrap up other important business, like calling the airline to check on your flight. In many hotels, you can also check out the night before or set up for an express checkout the following morning.

Even "last-minute" types should do everything in their power to force themselves to organize the night before. Once the wake-up call sounds on the morning of your departure, time has a tendency to fly like the wind!

97.
Don't Carry It...
Ship It

If, during the course of your vacation, it becomes apparent that you're going to be overburdened with luggage, consider shipping some of it. It may cost a little more, but it can save you wear and tear on your muscles and make navigating the airport and ride home more manageable.

Why not ship home that suitcase of dirty clothes? As long as you pack up only clothing that you brought with you from the United States and write on the package, "American goods returned," you won't have to pay duty.

Inexpensive gifts can also be shipped home—as long as their value does not exceed fifty dollars. To do this, you must send the package to a friend (you cannot send it to yourself, or you will be charged duty). You must also be sure to write on the package, "Unsolicited gift," what the gift is, and its value. In fact, you can do this a few times over the course of your trip—as long as you don't send more than fifty dollars worth of articles to the same friend in one day. Honesty is important here, so be truthful about what you are sending and its value. Your package will probably be checked.

If you do consider shipping your belongings, be obsessive about marking everything clearly. Use indelible, permanent ink, and make sure you affix exactly the right amount of postage.

98.

Hello, Airport
Gift Shop!

Some travelers do all of their souvenir shopping at airport gift shops. The higher cost doesn't bother them because it ends up being more convenient. They think, why carry souvenirs around on your vacation if you can just buy them before getting on the plane?

Duty-free shops at the airport can be a shopper's delight—but understand that the items available for purchase there aren't always discounted, they are just tax-free. Still, some airports sell popular perfumes, cigars, liquors, watches—even caviar—at great prices, so it's worthwhile to investigate.

There's a vast opportunity for souvenir hunters at airports all over the world. You're likely to have a long wait at the airport anyway—arriving early and waiting through security checks for your flight—so why not just accept the fact that it's going to cost a little more and use that waiting time to shop till you drop…into your seat on the plane?

99.

Your
Vacation Scrapbook

While you're enjoying your vacation, it's a great idea to keep in the back of your mind at all times the fact that you're going to assemble a vacation scrapbook when you return home. Each day that you set out while on vacation, leave a little extra room in your day pack for collecting everything and anything that you find for your vacation scrapbook. If you visit a fancy restaurant, grab a book of matches or a napkin printed with the restaurant's logo. Take free brochures offered at tourist locations—they usually contain photographs that can be clipped out and pasted in later. Keep the ticket stubs from every museum or show that you see, and try to purchase at least one interesting postcard from every place that you visit. Candy wrappers and advertisements for movies in other languages—even foreign newspapers or magazines can later be used for adding interesting touches to your scrapbook. Take everything that you can fit for one day, and then go through your collection back at your hotel room and weed out the things that you won't use.

When you return home, visit a craft store to find all of the products that you need to create a truly superior memento. Then put the book together. You may want to ask your spouse or children for help. Making scrapbooks together always brings families closer —as does looking through those scrapbooks year after year and reliving your vacation all over again!

100.

Home at Last...
I Could Use a Vacation!

Going on vacation is *exhausting*! It's also fun and exciting. But planning a vacation, leaving for vacation, experiencing a vacation, and then coming home from that vacation can wipe you out to the point where you need another vacation!

While it's great to come home after being away for a period of time, it remains difficult to return to normal life right away. There's always that grace period after a trip where you need to wind down, regroup, and remember what home life is like. Plus you're almost always eager to do three things within a half hour of being home: drop off your film, get your mail, and tell someone about your trip.

When you step through your front door upon returning home, spend a little time relaxing. Leave the bags for a while, and just sit. Give yourself a chance to exhale. You'll be tempted to check your phone messages and then call everyone you know—you want to find out what went on while you were gone and tell them about the great time you had. But try to resist that urge. Leave the catching up until tomorrow, when you won't be so tired.

Instead of calling each person on your list to give them the vacation overview, consider sending a mass e-mail announcing your return home. Include the highlights and lowlights of your trip, as well as how much you missed them all.

Finally, when you find yourself feeling melancholy or nostalgic and wondering how your trip flew by, that's the time to throw a party! Invite all of your friends over to see your vacation photographs, look through your scrapbook, and listen to some of your most memorable vacation moments as recorded in your journal.

Prepare for the mixed emotions that you'll have upon coming home. Then you'll be better able to work around them and reflect on your vacation as the special, relaxing time away that it was meant to be.